CHARLES COOPER

The Last Emigrant Ship

by

Michael Stammers

NATIONAL MUSEUMS & GALLERIES ON MERSEYSIDE

NMGM

NATIONAL MUSEUMS & GALLERIES ON MERSEYSIDE

2003

Published 2003
by
National Museums & Galleries on Merseyside,
Merseyside Maritime Museum,
Albert Dock, Liverpool L3 4AQ.

British Library Cataloguing-in-Publication Data
A catalogue record of this book is available from the British Library

ISBN 1 902700 22 8

Typeset by Milepost Research,
41 Fountain Street, Accrington BB5 0QR.

CONTENTS

The **James Monroe**, *the pioneer American Packet Ship of 1817 arriving at Liverpool.*

The Trustees of NMGM

The **Charles Cooper** *under full sail in a contemporary painting.*

Private Collection, New York

Chapter 1: INTRODUCTION

I first visited the *Charles Cooper* in Stanley, Falkland Islands, in 1978. I had been invited to join the South Street Seaport's survey to document American-built sailing vessels surviving in the Falkland Islands. This was supported by the National Endowment for the Humanities. The prime objective was to document the hulk of the *Charles Cooper* — the only surviving mid-19th century American packet ship — for the Maine State Museum. South Street Seaport Museum was still in its visionary stage and had acquired the hulk of the *Charles Cooper* from the Falkland Islands Company in 1968 with a view to bringing a large section back for restoration and display at New York. Unfortunately, this ambition was never achieved.

The survey was led by Norman Brouwer who had already visited the Falklands. Norman is one of the world's greatest experts on 19th century sailing vessels. He was supported by Hilton Matthews, a shipwright from the Isle of Wight, who had been working on another of South Street's acquisitions, the iron full–rigged ship *Wavertree*. Hilton was also a diver and took on responsibility for collating and drafting the measurements gathered for preparing the lines of the *Charles Cooper*. The late Peter Throckmorton, one of the pioneers of nautical archaeology, was another important member of the party. He, along with Eric Berryman then of the University of New Mexico, took responsibility for the making of a silicone rubber mould from the *Charles Cooper*'s stern carving. These two also organised the recovery of a forty foot section of the hull of the *St Mary* wrecked at Pleasant Roads in 1890 for the Maine State Museum. This core team was supplemented by volunteers including Avery Stone and Nathaniel Greene, Joseph Sawtelle, George Cooper and Rufus Jefferson, plus the crew of the visiting yacht *Jennie Wren*. Their hard work and ingenuity made an important contribution to the amount of data that was gathered.

The project also needed the active co-operation of the people of the Falklands. John Smith was the key person. In 1978, John worked for the Falkland Islands Company. In his spare time, he ran the Falklands Museum with Joan Spruce in the end bay of the FIC offices at Crozier place. John had also been involved in historic ship recording when the late Karl Kortum visited Stanley in 1966, and John produced the first detailed description of the *Charles Cooper* and her condition. He eventually became the first full-time curator of the Falklands Museum and continued to be an influential figure in the drive to record and conserve Stanley's unique heritage of 19th century sailing ships. I must also thank David Eynon of South Atlantic Marine Services. David's workshops and gallery overlook the Charles Cooper and over the years he has been a tremendous supporter as well as providing boats and underwater photography. He is also an important figure on the Falkland Island's Committee on the Wrecks.

Merseyside Maritime Museum was established in 1980, and in 1987 was able to find the resources to carry out the recording of the hulk of the barque *Jhelum* which had been built at Liverpool in 1849. We were able to carry out survey work and repairs to the roof of the *Charles Cooper*, and to continue monitoring the condition through the 1990s. Unfortunately, the deterioration of the hull has been speeded up since about 1998 by marine boring gribble and teredo worms. The end may be in sight because the remains of the hull with a mass of loose timbers could be a shipping hazard. Therefore it is time to write a complete account of this important vessel's history. Although the archive created through our efforts in 1978 is safely stored at South Street Seaport and Norman Brouwer has written some excellent articles, there has been no complete account of this important vessel.

I am grateful to Norman for letting me have copies of material held at South Street and to Nicholas Dean of Edgcomb, Maine for additional material. Nicholas is another Falkland hand who was involved in the recovery of the bow of the American extreme clipper *Snow Squall* as well as being the author of an excellent recent book on the ship. I must also thank another resident of Maine, Huston Dodge, who prepared the midships cross section of the ship. Thanks also to Jane Cameron, the Falklands Government Archivist, and her assistant, Tansy Newman, who made the records of the Falkland Islands Government and the Company available for my last research visit in 2002. These filled an important gap in the story and, in particular, the history of the *Charles Cooper* as a hulk in Stanley harbour. This research would not have been possible without the generous support of the Shackleton Foundation. May I also thank their committee for their patience because I had to put off this work for over two years after receiving the grant. I must also thank the Trustees of National Museums and Galleries on Merseyside for their continuing support for a research project in islands far away from Liverpool, and my colleagues John Kearon, Jim Forrester (now Imperial War Museum) and Paul Browne for their support in our various expeditions from 1987 to 1998, Graham Usher, furniture conservator for identifying the timbers and finally to my secretary Kathy Davies for dealing with this manuscript.

The **Charles Cooper** *at Stanley, Falkland Islands, as an abandoned hulk in 1987.*

Chapter 2: DESIGN AND CONSTRUCTION OF THE *CHARLES COOPER*

The New York Herald published the following small news item in its issue for the 11th of November 1856: *'Launch: Mr.Wm Hall will launch this morning at 10 o'clock, from his yard at Black Rock, Connecticut, the ship Charles Cooper, of 1000 tons register. She is intended for Messrs Laytin & Hurlbut's line of Antwerp packets and will be commanded by Capt. G. N. Lamb'.*

William Hall appears not to have been a regular builder of packet vessels. He may have been the Hall of the firm of shipbuilders known as Hall and Teaque of Black Rock who launched the 1579 ton clipper **Black Hawk** on their account in 1854. Black Rock and the area west of the Connecticut River was not noted for building large ships unlike the yards on the Connecticut and Mystic Rivers.[1] Although the *Charles Cooper* was an exceptional vessel for Black Rock, it was only one of 306 ships and barques completed in the United States in 1856 and with these there were also 103 brigs, 594 schooners, 479 sloops or canal boats and 221 steamers.[2] However, the *Charles Cooper* was also exceptional as a packet ship. Of the total of 185 ships listed by Robert Albion in the first serious history of American packets — *Square Riggers on Schedule,* published in 1938 — 160 were built in New York and only 24 in New England.[3]

The American mercantile marine was at its zenith and its packet ships dominated the Transatlantic trade. There were regular and reliable steamship services and new operators added more sailings in the mid 1850s. These were operated largely under the Red Ensign, and the most successful, the British and North American Steam Navigation Company (later known as the Cunard Line) operated with a government subsidy for carrying the mail. There was also the American-owned Collins Line, which ran large and luxurious wooden paddle steamers between 1850 and 1858. Ship technology was improving rapidly with iron hulls, screw propulsion, improved boilers operating at high pressures and compound engines. The *Charles Cooper* was at the end of the line. The outbreak of the American Civil War in 1861 and the resulting Confederate campaign against Federal merchant ships permanently damaged the merchant shipping of the United States and the last sailing packets ceased to run their regular voyages across the Atlantic in the late 1860s.

Packet ships or boats were originally vessels plying between two ports on a regular basis with mail and possibly passengers and premium goods. The rise in the American-European packet trade after the War of 1812 gave employment to merchant ships of greater size than any others except East Indiamen. The establishment of the Black Ball Line with the sailing of the *James Monroe* on 5th January 1818 from New York bound for Liverpool is usually seen as the starting point of the 'packet ship era'. The proprietors promised a monthly service sailing on a set day whether the vessel was full or not. The requirements of the packet ship made cargo capacity desirable because the Transatlantic trade required the carriage of all kinds of goods. Outward from New York this might include cotton, flour and all kinds of American produce and on the return leg there were European manufactures especially British ones including machinery, textiles and luxury goods. There were also passengers and the poorer travellers (many emigrating in search of a better life) could be accommodated in

---

1   W A Fairburn, *Merchant Sail*, Lovell, Maine, 1955
2   S Boorsch in her unpublished paper for South Street Seaport Museum of 1970, 1.
3   H I Chapelle, *The National Watercraft Collection,* Washington, 1960, 29.

the swept out tween-decks of packet ships. *'The stormy North Atlantic and the hard winter passages combined with the desire for speedy passages, made the power to carry sail in heavy weather, seaworthiness, strength and reliability prime requisites. Though the business was profitable, it was never one that produced tremendous profits; this prevented the rapid development in design and the appearance of extremely sharp models. The desire for speed was slowly gaining strength and the packets gradually felt its effect. A great part of the profits of the Trans-Atlantic packet trade were obtained from the passenger traffic, and this was a factor in the design and construction and fitting of this class of ship'.*[4] This evolution can be seen in the increasing tonnage and length of packet ships and the gradual change in hull shape. There was also fierce competition between the shipbuilders. The best imported recent British works on naval architecture and generally adopted a more scientific approach to their designs. This in turn led to home grown works starting with the publication of Laughlin MacKay's *Practical Shipbuilder* in 1839. This was later followed by the foundation of a technical journal, the *Nautical Magazine* and the publication of further influential works especially those of J W Griffiths.[5] However McKay and his fellow pioneers of new designs were a minority. This was because the American tonnage measurement rules (introduced in 1789 on similar lines to the British Old Measurement and not reformed until 1864) favoured short deep ships.[6]

The pioneer vessel, the **James Monroe**, had been built by A. Brown at New York in 1817, measured 424 tons, and was 118 feet long with a beam of 28 feet and a depth of hold of 14 feet. Nearly twenty years later, the **Oxford** built by William Webb at New York for the Dramatic Line of New York–Le Havre packets were much bigger — 752 tons, 147 feet 6 inches long, 33 feet 6 inches beam and 21 feet 6 inches depth of hold. Webb's packet the **Yorkshire** of 1843 measured 996 tons and was 166 feet 6 inches long, 36 feet beam and 21 feet depth of hold.[7] The **Charles Cooper** was of similar dimensions to the **Yorkshire** — 977 tons, 166 feet long, 35 feet 10 inches beam, but less depth in the hold — 17 feet 11 inches — 3 feet less than the **Yorkshire**. This might be because the owner's main business was in coastal packets to Mobile, the Gulf ports of Florida and New Orleans. They all had problems with shallow entrances.

The first packets were general traders that were strongly built and that were known to sail well. Early on packets began to be built that were larger and stronger than the conventional vessel. While demand for their services was increasing, competition between rival lines was fierce and speed became a factor. Packets were recognised as special vessels even by laymen and even as early as the 1820s. Daniel Constable in New York wrote to his relatives in Sussex in 1823: *'Thursday 27 [February] hard frost, cold wind, clear sky to launch the Canada a superb ship of 6.00 tons for one of the Liverpool line of paketts, for the first time in my life I was on board a launch, it was on the East River about two miles above the Battery, the river is I think a mile wide, she glided beautifully into her own element, in attendance was a steam boat to haul her down to a warf to be rigged, the whole a very pretty spectacle, in her spacious cabin, uninvited and without ceremonie I drew up my chair and partook of a dinner with the owners, builder, Captain and friends…'*[8]

This kind of scene and celebratory meal doubtless accompanied the launching of the **Charles Cooper**. Daniel Constable went back to the **Canada** just before sailing for Liverpool: *'I have just been on board her, her accommodations are indeed most splendid, I do think they surpass anything I have seen in a merchant ship, the cabin decorations are most costly, a profusion of rich carving and guilding, elegant furniture &c, I have pleasure in contemplating the good and useful works of this young nation, considering how youthful they are they do a great many cleaver things'.*[9]

Constable, though thoroughly biased in favour of all things American, was right. The

---

4   H L Chapelle, *History of American Sailing Ships*, London,1936,277-8.

5   J. W. Griffiths, *The Shipbuilder's Manual and Referee*, New York, 1853 and, *A Treatise on marine and naval architecture as theory and practice blended in shipbuilding*, London,1857.

6   D M MacGregor, *Fast Sailing Ships Their Design and Construction, 1775-1875* 2nd edition, London, 1988, 154.

7   D R MacGregor, *Merchant Sailing Ships*, London, 1984, 166-7. Depth of hold is the inside depth used for assessing volume and from that tonnage. It is not the same as the draught to the bottom of its keel.

8   J B Jenkins, *Citizen Daniel (1775-1835) and the Call of America*, Hartford,Conn., 2000, 290.

9   J B Jenkins, 298

*Left: The **Charles Cooper**'s hull was heavily reinforced with wooden brackets (knees).*

*Below: These contrasted with the British shipbuilders' increasing use of iron straps and knees for internal strengthening, as seen on the barque **Vicar of Bray** of 1841.*

Bottom: This aerial view taken after the roof was stripped off in 2001 shows the shape of the hull and the layout of the main deck beams. Photocopy supplied by D Eynon, original not traced.

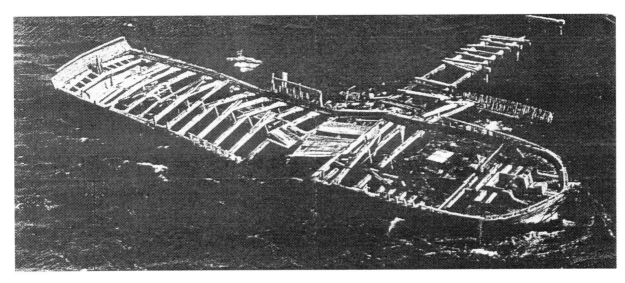

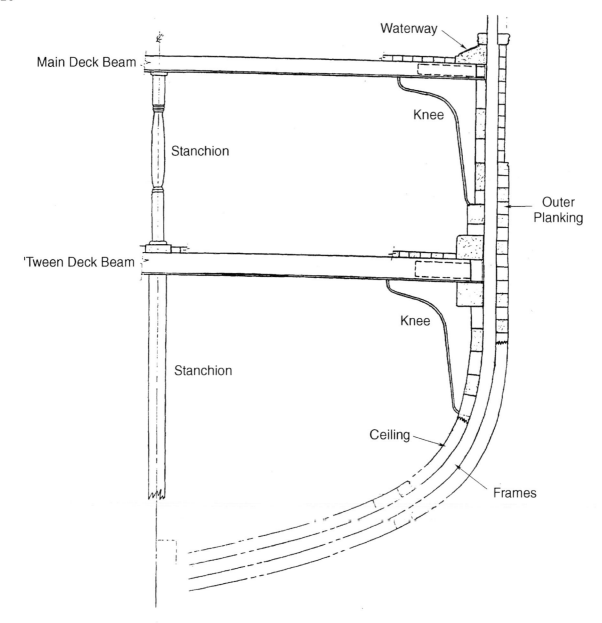

The **Charles Cooper***'s cross section at Deck Beam 11, counting from the bow.*

Don Meissner

American packets came to dominate the Atlantic trade until they were displaced by the power of the steamer and the threat of Confederate capture in the American Civil War (1861-65).

Increasing the size of wooden hulls and increasing the sail area brought with them some difficult technical problems. Longer hulls which were necessary for greater speed and capacity would inevitably hog and sag in the heavy Atlantic swells. They had to be strengthened by additional timbering. The size of the keel and the keelson had to be increased. The keelson was paired with the keel as the main longitudinal strength member, and was fastened over the floors (bottom frames). In the case of the *Charles Cooper*, both keel and keelson are buried deep in mud and rock. The overall length of the hull meant that it must have been substantial. To give some idea, the clipper *Mastiff* which was built at Boston in 1856 and was slightly larger at 1,030 tons than the *Charles Cooper* had a keel of rock maple measuring 14 inches by 26.[10]

Snow Squall of 1851 which was another hulk in Falkland Islands and of similar dimensions had a keelson with three rider keelsons on top of it and two sister keelsons alongside it. The

10   W L Crothers, *The American–built Clipper Ship 1850-56*, Camden, Maine,1997, 34

keelson itself measures 12 inches by 12 inches as do the sister keelsons and the topmost rider keelson. All told they amount to a girder 3 feet deep running the whole length of the hull.[11] It is likely that there were more longitudinal strength members fastened at the turn of the bilge. Again if we use the *Mastiff* as a yardstick, there were bilge keelsons on each side, 14 inches square plus stringers measuring 8 inches square.[12] The stem and stern post are attached to the keel at each end and measure about 15 inches square at their tops. There would have been a series of deadwoods attached to them to allow the cant frames (the end ones where the hull comes to a point) to be fastened. All these are buried.

The floors which form the bottom of the hull framing may have measured as much as 15 by 12 inches as was the case in the *Mastiff*.[13] The upper part of the frames measure on average 9 inches wide by 7 inches deep. These are paired as was the common practice with 6 inch gaps between the pairs. The choice of timber was another critical factor in the overall strength of the ship. British critics of the time condemned North American built vessels as 'softwood' ships. While it cannot be denied that American woods do not have the ultimate strength of English oak, nevertheless there were some excellent varieties of ship timber available to the American builders. Moreover the timber was available in large sections. English vessels of the same era relied to a much greater extent on internal iron reinforcement for their strength. A comparison between the *Charles Cooper* and the British-built barque the *Vicar of Bray* shows the differing approaches. The *Charles Cooper*'s frames were made of American chestnut (castanea dentata) which flourished in the eastern United States from the Great Lakes to Alabama. *'The wood is semi-hard, dense, tough and strong; it can be worked well with tools and takes a beautiful finish. While suitable for shipbuilding, chestnut saw minimal use due to the abundance of the superior white oak. It was, however, quite acceptable for the construction of ship frames'.*[14] In comparative strength white oak was rated as 100 as against 68 for chestnut. This could be taken to mean that the *Charles Cooper* was a rather inferior vessel. As a counter to this the heavy scantling of the timbers and the quality of the build was such that there can be little doubt that the hull was fit for its purpose. Its survival first as a floating hulk and later as a beached storehouse at Stanley is also witness of the quality of materials and build. The chestnut still retains its spring and smell beneath the battered exterior of the frames even after almost 150 years. It is also worth pointing out that it is uncertain what the buried lower frames were made from; perhaps they were white oak. The only major vessel that has been discovered to included chestnut in its frames was the 1679 ton clipper ship *Andrew Jackson* of 1855 which was also built in Connecticut on the Mystic River.[15]

The frames connected with further longitudinal strength members which ran the whole length of the ship. A beam shelf supported the tween deck beams with the clamp on top, and were made from Norway pine (pinus resinosa). While light, grained and rather soft with a strength rating of 60, it was suitable for interior components. It also had good resistance to rot and where it has not been exposed to the marine borers remains in good shape to this day. The waterway which was the equivalent to clamp on the main deck is a massive chamfered component and was fashioned from live oak (quercus virginiana). This wood as the name suggests was first discovered on the Virginia coast. In fact it can be grown as far south as Texas. Its strength rating was 149, the strongest of the American shipbuilding woods and this demonstrates that Hall was putting strength into the hull where it was most needed. However, the choice of live oak is unusual because it does not lend itself to straight lengths.

---

11 N Dean, *Snow Squall The Last American Clipper Ship,* Bath, Maine, 2001, 281.

12 W L Crothers, 203.

13 W L Crothers, 146.

14 W L Crothers, 24.

15 W N Patterson, *Mystic Built,* Mystic, Conn., 1989, 12 quotes Henry Hall's *Report on the Ship-building Industry of the U. S.* of 1882 on the materials used in Mystic yards before 1861 'Native timber was used largely; the state being well stocked with oak and chestnut, but pitch-pine and southern oak were used when the local timber gave out'.

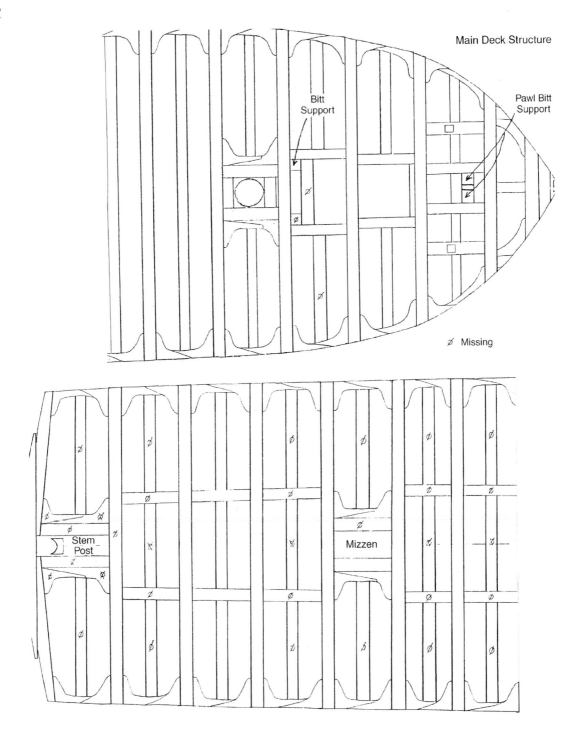

The bow and stern main deck structure.

N Brouwer

There were two skins of planking attached to the frames. The outer strakes are of Norway pine and measured 6 inches in width by 5 inches deep and fastened by wooden treenails of black locust (Robinia pseudo-acacia). It is a small tough tree found in the Appalachian mountains. It is difficult to work with hand tools but turns well and was ideal for making treenails — the wooden pins for fastening the outer planking. The inner planking, the ceiling was also cut from Norway pine measuring 13 inches wide by 6 inches thick. Unlike the outer planking this was fastened by iron spikes.

The main and tween deck beams are massive baulks of Norway pine, measuring $13^1/_2$ inches wide and 7 inches deep. Between there are smaller section beams 9 inches wide and $5^1/_2$ inches deep cut from the same timber. The whole assembly is braced fore and aft by two lines of carlings which have the same dimensions as the secondary deck beams. There were also

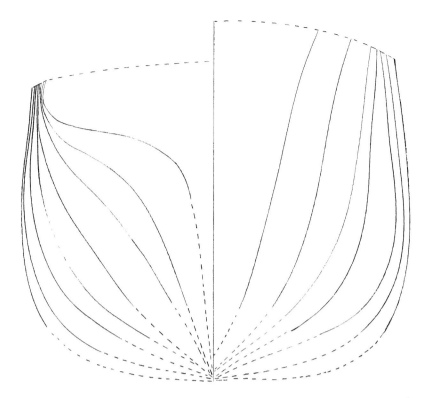

Body plan — the dotted lines indicate where the hull was buried and the likely shape.

Hilton Matthews

additional half beams and carlings at the bow between the first and second beams. The larger beams for both decks are braced by horizontal lodging knees and vertical knees. These are 'grown' timbers where the natural curve of the grain of the wood is preserved to ensure maximum strength. They are formed from hackmatack (larix laricina) and this is also known as tamarack or European larch. It is tough with a strength rating of 75 and the knees were cut from the base of the tree to utilise the bole and the root. It was grown all over the north eastern states. The planking on both decks is Norway pine $5^1/_2$ inches wide by $3^1/_2$ inches deep, and is fastened to the deck beams by iron spikes.

The deck beams are supported at their centres by stanchions. In the hold these vertical posts are simple squared pieces of timber which fastened by right angled iron knees. These are one of the few uses of iron reinforcement in the whole hull. The tween deck stanchions are handsome turned columns which are strengthened by an iron rod running down their centres. This had a threaded end so that it could be tightened up by screwing up a nut at the bottom. Other internal reinforcements were fitted at the bow and the stern–hooks which are huge horizontal reinforcing brackets and pointers which are diagonal reinforcing timbers for the same purpose.

The hull was sheathed to protect it from marine growth. The advertisement for the sale of five eighths of the shares in the New York *Journal of Commerce* of 15th February 1860 stated that it 'was coppered on her last voyage'. This might imply that the **Charles Cooper** was not sheathed at the time of her launch. This is unlikely, because American vessels were sheathed as a matter of course by this time. However metal sheathing did not last and had to be renewed. The compound sheathing of 60 percent copper and 40 percent zinc, the patent Muntz metal, had an expected useful life of forty months.[16] None of the sheathing has survived. It was probably stripped away either for re-use or as part of the attrition of lying as a hulk without significant maintenance from 1866. Some of the small copper tacks used for fastening are still present. The development of practical copper sheathing was a very important technical

---

16 N Dean, *The Snow Squall, The Last American Clipper Ship*, Bath, Maine, 2001, 35.

The massive internal construction of the transom. The huge 15 inch square transom beam at the top can be seen behind the row of 'tween deck stanchions.

The carved trail boards were still in place in 1949. Note the original corrugated iron roof. It was replaced by aluminium which lasted until 2001.

Gerald Roberts

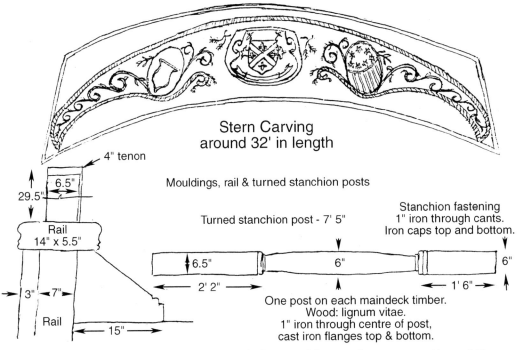

Stern Carving
around 32' in length

Mouldings, rail & turned stanchion posts

Turned stanchion post - 7' 5"

Stanchion fastening
1" iron through cants.
Iron caps top and bottom.

4" tenon

6.5"

29.5"

Rail
14" x 5.5"

3" 7"

Rail

15"

6.5"

2' 2"

6"

1' 6"

6"

One post on each maindeck timber.
Wood: lignum vitae.
1" iron through centre of post,
cast iron flanges top & bottom.

A field sketch of the stern carving, the 'tween deck stanchion and a cross section of the main deck waterway, 1978.

The late Nat Greene — volunteer on the 1978 expedition

Part of the restored trail board displayed in the Falklands Museum.

advance for wooden sailing ships. The copper not only protected ships' bottoms from sea worm but also prevented or delayed marine growth. A clean underwater hull could maintain speed and would not need frequent dry docking for cleaning and thus reduce maintenance costs. Copper fastenings were used to fasten the butt ends of planks that were sheathed to ensure there was no electrolytic action.

While the hull structure of packet ships developed and became more complex to cope with the added stress of increasing size, the shape changed as well. As already mentioned there was great competition between the leading designers to produce a form that was speedy but with retaining good capacity. William Webb believed his packet *Yorkshire* of 1843 was that 'happy combination'. This was of similar dimensions to the *Charles Cooper* except for a greater depth. It enshrined the main characteristics of the later packet ships 'a full midships section, good length of body combined with fine ends '[17]

There was a great deal of this thinking in the form of the *Charles Cooper* which has a short but hollow entrance and a fairly short run. The floors are not as flat as those of the *Yorkshire* and many of the later packets. Though advertised as 'a clipper ship' the *Charles Cooper* was built for cargo capacity rather than speed and certainly, the voyage times were not faster than average.

The *Charles Cooper*, like many American–built sailing ships of the 1850s had a beautiful hull. It is still possible to see this in its shattered remains. The bow is slightly raked and gently curves outwards at the top. At its full extent it would have projected forward with carved trail boards leading into a figurehead. An unlabelled sketch in a personal log kept by the second mate, Franklin Jordan, in 1862 showed a male figure holding a wand with a star on it.[18] One of these trail boards is displayed in the Falklands Museum. It is an elegant piece of carving based on a leaf motif inspired by the Neo-classical style to be found in many land-based decoration in the 1850s. There was also a sweeping sheer rising to the bow with a good seaworthy look to it. This was a feature of American ships at a time when equivalent British 'frigate-built' ships had little or no sheer. Aft, there is a gently curved transom which is also cambered. This structure is supported on one massive transom beam, measuring 15 inches square. This not only extended the area of the aft accommodation but also provided reserve buoyancy. The transom is also the place for the main carving on the ship — a most elaborate stern board. This was an important decorative feature on many American sailing ships of the *Charles Cooper*'s era. This one is particularly elaborate with three oval shields embracing curling leaves of similar design to the trail boards and rope work. The shield on the starboard side features the stars and stripes; while the other two remain unidentified. The only contemporary painting of the *Charles Cooper* shows 'painted ports' along the sides of the hull.

---

17 H L Chapelle, *The National Watercraft Collection*, 28.

18 N Brouwer 'The 1856 Packet *Charles Cooper*' in *Seaport*, vol.15 (1981), 21

The stern carving in situ in 1978. The projecting timbers and iron rails are the start of an access platform to remove the carving to the safety of the Falklands Museum.

This was a broad band of white on a black hull with black oblong shapes at regular intervals. It is said to have originated by British merchant vessels imitating the paint scheme of Royal Navy warships at the beginning of the 19th century. It was a sort of camouflage to make pirates think twice about attacking. It carried on as a form of decoration that enhanced the beauty of the ship right into the time of steel four–masted barques. For example, the *Archibald Russell* of 1905, one of the last ever built, had painted ports. It was unusual for American ships which tended to have all black hulls on the outside with white deck houses and rails. Time and weather have eroded all the exterior paint work. It is likely that the lower masts and the deckhouse were painted white. A tiny section of blue was found on the waterway near the bowsprit. Blue was a common colour for the waterways with the deck themselves left unpainted but well scrubbed.

Only a few fittings have survived from the *Charles Cooper*'s main deck. Much of the lay-out disappeared when the hulk was fitted with a roof. The painting comes to the rescue because this shows the major items from a small raised forecastle, a large deck house aft of the fore mast, boats on skids forward of the mizzen mast and a raised trunk and half poop aft which was a fairly standard plan. Working aft from the bow, there was the windlass for the anchors with its pawls, cable stoppers and pump action. The latter was one of the technical innovations introduced by a number of patents in the early 19th century. It could raise the anchors far more quickly than the traditional method which employed hand spikes. This survives along with one detached cathead. There is a small hatch and then the mast partners of the foremast and these are reinforced by pairs of lodging knees. Part of the port side of fore bitts has survived. Immediately aft of the fore mast, there was once a long deck house which is illustrated in the painting. In other packet ships such as the *Isaac Webb* of 1850, this accommodated two galleys (one for the crew and the steerage passengers and for the officers and the first class passengers) and possibly second class cabins for some of the senior members of the crew such as the sailmaker and the carpenter.[19] The crew lived in the forward end of the tween decks with access via the forward hatch. Abaft the deck house was the main hatch and the two pumps and their well going down to the bilges was immediately abaft the main mast. None of these features have survived. The boats were stowed aft of the pumps. The aft hatch was situated below the boats and that survives. On other packet ships, this was fitted with a portable companion way to allow access to the steerage accommodation in the tween decks. On voyages where only cargo was carried, this would be removed and the hatched battened down with canvas tarpaulins in the normal fashion. This was followed by another deck house which has been removed. This trunk cabin has two figures standing on it in the painting. This

19 C. G. Davis, *American Sailing Ships Their Plans and History*, New York, c. 1930, 62-63.

Fore Deck layout.
Norman Brouwer

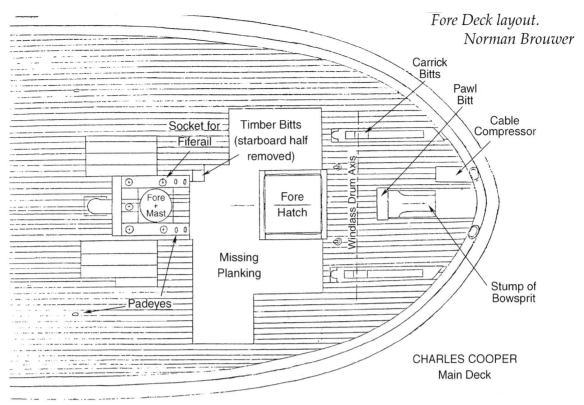

Carrick Bitts
Pawl Bitt
Cable Compressor
Socket for Fiferail
Timber Bitts (starboard half removed)
Fore + Mast
Fore Hatch
Windlass Drum Axis
Missing Planking
Padeyes
Stump of Bowsprit

CHARLES COOPER
Main Deck

Above: Taken in 2002, this photograph clearly shows the stump of the bowsprit, the windlass, fore hatch bitts and the stumps of the bulwark stanchions.

Above: The cable stopper; the patentee's name 'C Perley' and 'Patent 1824' was cast into its top, but is now much eroded.

Left: A close up of the windlass.

and the whole aft section was devoted to accommodating the master, the officers and the first class passengers. The layout of the accommodation will be considered in the next chapter. The figure at the wheel right aft in the painting shows that there was a raised deck — a half poop — and this probably ran from the transom to half way along the trunk cabin. All these features have been removed but the evidence of the painting and the common practice of American ships of the time suggest that this description is probably correct. The bulwarks on American ships which protect the main deck were normally quite high and carried a pin rail for belaying running rigging. Several cut down uprights have survived along with two cleats which were probably used for the mooring lines.[20] There are also a number of lead-lined scupper pipes that have been cut through the waterways to help the main deck of water.

Not much of the *Charles Cooper*'s masts and rigging have survived; but the fragments combined with the details of the painting and contemporary practice can give a fairly clear idea. Although the ship was only on the larger side of medium, for there were American clippers of double the tonnage, the size of the masts and spars is still marvellously big. The *Charles Cooper* was a full rigged ship, with three masts and a bowsprit. Only the heel of the bowsprit survives along with the three sets of mast partners which indicate the size and position of the three masts. The surviving piece of bowsprit is a huge squared piece of red pine, measuring 28 by 27 inches and is the final witness to the massive size of the masts and spars.

Starting at the bow, the bowsprit came in two sections: the bowsprit proper with the longer jib-boom and flying jib-boom on top. These latter spars were usually one continuous timber by the 1850s. They could be hauled in if necessary when in a crowded port. They were supported by a complex system of stays which were spread below by the romantically named dolphin striker. There were more stays on each side which ran back to the hull. These spars also carried the fore stays of the main mast and there were triangular fore sails on three of these. These sails — the fore staysail, inner and outer jibs — were fastened by iron rings and could be hoisted from the fore deck. They were furled on top of the jib boom. The crew could get to the end of the jib boom using foot ropes, but this was very hazardous in gales when hands could be swept off and drowned as the bow plunged into the raging waves. The fore and the main mast s were built in three sections — lower, top and topgallant — and carried five yards; fore course or main, upper and lower topsails, topgallant and royal. The topsail had been one sail since its introduction in the 15th century. By the 1840s it had grown to be such a deep cumbersome sail as ships became bigger that various patents were taken out to improve its handling. Cunningham's, a British one of 1850, involved roller reefing. Forbes, an American captain split the topsail into two sails with the topmast fidded abaft the lower mast in 1841. This was modified by another American, Howe, in 1853 with the split sail and the topmast in its usual position ahead of the lower mast. This became standard for both the British and American merchant ships and the *Charles Cooper* was fitted in this way. The painting also shows studding sails on both masts. These were fair weather sails which could be set on light spars extending out from the yards. The mizzen mast was similar though shorter and had a single topsail and a fore and aft sail, the spanker supported by a gaff and a boom on the aft side of the mast. Between the masts there were also more stay sails like those running up from the bowsprit.

The masts stepped on the keelson and their positions can still be identified by the mast partners on the tween and main decks. The huge weight of masts, yards and canvas and the stresses from the motions of the sea and the forces of the wind called for substantial supporting rigging. the fore and aft stays have already been mentioned. The shrouds ran from the hounds (the upper section) of the lower masts to each side of the hull. There were probably five or six.

---

20 The speculative parts of the *Charles Cooper's* layout rely a great deal on Crothers' comparative study of American clipper ships' deck layouts. His work is based on 152 examples built between 1850 and 1856. While there are many variations, there are many standard features such as a small topgallant forecastle, the position of the main hatch and the pumps etc. W L Crothers, 383-420.

The upper masts had their own smaller shrouds running plus back stays. The latter ran to the sides of the ship. It is not clear whether the standing rigging was made from hemp or wire. The former was more common in American ships, while the British vessels such as the *Jhelum* adopted the stronger but less flexible iron wire rope. Nothing survives of the standing rigging beyond some of the iron chainplates on the port side. These were anchors for the deadeyes — sheaveless blocks with three holes which made them look like a skull — and these were use to adjust the setting of the shrouds and the stays. There were miles of rope and hundreds of blocks to control the sails. There were halliards (haul yards) for hoisting sails, braces and lifts for controlling the angles of the yards, sheets and tacks for controlling the set of the sails and clew lines, bunt lines, down hauls etc for drawing in or lowering the sails, reef tackles and reef points for reducing the area of certain key sails, brails for taking in the spanker etc. The final stow had to be carried out by the crew who used the shrouds to climb the masts and then went out on the yards on foot ropes. Every rope had its own position down on the deck. There were fife rails on each side of each mast and pin rails along the bulwarks. These were drilled with holes to receive large wooden belaying pins on which the running rigging could be checked and coiled down. The sails were of cotton canvas which was very hard on the finger nails compared with the flax canvas favoured by British ships. Much of the crew's work revolved around a never ending round of maintenance to the sails and the rigging and this involved the acquisition of a wide range of rope working and sail sewing skills.[21] All that survives of this complex network is a large cleat which had a fairlead for the fore course sheet — the rope controlling the bottom corner of the sail.

Right: The remains of the fore bitts. Note the dead eye for either the main or main topmast stays.

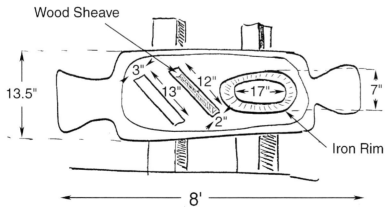

Left: A sketch of the last surviving cleat for handling the fore course sheet.

John Smith, Stanley

---

21   Apologies to any sailing ship experts for this simplified account. Those interested in the detail of masting and rigging and working a square rigged sailing ship should refer to R. Kipping, *Sails and Sailmaking*, 1st edition London, 1858, and his *Masting, Mast-Making and Rigging of Ships*, 10th edition, London, 1858, H A Underhill, *Masting and Rigging the Clipper ship and Ocean Carrier*, Glasgow, 1946.

*The bustle of the packet wharves of New York is reflected in this wood cut from Harper's Weekly which was much the same scene as when the **Charles Cooper** first loaded for Antwerp.*

South Street Seaport Museum

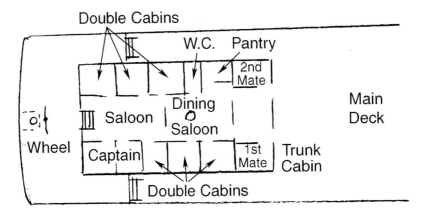

Based on other American-built ships of the period, this may have been the layout of the first class accommodation which would have inevitably been at the stern of the ship.

Chapter 3: ON A REGULAR ROUTE, LAYTIN & HURLBUT's ANTWERP PACKET SERVICE

The *Charles Cooper* was registered at New York on 11th January 1857. There were seven shareholders. Edwin Hurlbut and William Laytin were the main shareholders and the managers. They held seven sixteenths. Shares in ships were divided into multiples of four up to sixty-four by custom and practice.

Charles Cooper of New York held two. William Hall, the shipbuilder and Thomas Rawson, a Connecticut business associate held four. Munson Hawley of Bridgeport, Connecticut, James Phillips of New Orleans and George Lamb, the ship's master held a sixteenth each. It was common for both the shipbuilder and the master to hold a stake in a new vessel. In William Hall's case, this investment may have been an attempt to recoup the loss he suffered when his new clipper the *Black Hawk* built on his own account sank on the first voyage. Shipbuilding was a competitive, hand to mouth kind of business and not all shipbuilders were good business men. Even the great Boston shipbuilder, Donald McKay, who had the finest of reputations, got into financial difficulties from time to time. It is unclear just who the Charles Cooper was who gave his name to this new ship. Boorsch's research suggests that the most likely candidate was the merchant of that name whose offices were at 27 South Street. However the New York *Journal of Commerce* for 15th February 1860 carried an advertisement for the sale of the *Charles Cooper* which asked interested parties to 'apply to CHARLES COOPER at the office of Laytin & Hurlbut, 84 South Street'. This surely implied that the man Charles Cooper was a working member of the firm and not a business associate with his own enterprise. This is an alternative explanation for the naming of the vessel. James Phillips does not appear to have been Hurlbut & Laytin's agent at New Orleans, and so it is impossible to identify his connection with the firm. The same applies to Munson Hawley. Shipowning partnerships were normally built up from family or business links where there was trust between the investor (the silent partners) and the managing owners. There was some protection for the silent investors against fraud or loss because they would only be responsible to the extent of their shareholding and there was an element of limited liability as a result of a measure passed by the New York Legislature in 1832.[22] Shipping shares though not without risk (remember William Hall's *Black Hawk* disaster) had paid well in the early 1850s. After the shipping boom that had started with the discovery of gold in California in 1849 U.S. trade had levelled off by 1855. There was some in the next two years but by 1857 there was a full scale depression with as many as 800 ships laid up at New York for lack of cargoes.[23] In the optimistic early 1850s many new ships had been ordered and further ones built on speculation. To make matters worse for the packet shipowners, the number of Atlantic steamer lines had increased. Between 1850 and 1856, twenty-eight Transatlantic steam ventures had been launched. Many failed after a single voyage. The successful ones included the Collins Line, the New York and Havre Steam Navigation Company, and the Inman Line in 1850; the Allan Line (to Canada) 1854; the Anchor Line, and the Hamburg America Line in 1856. The New York and Havre Steam Navigation

---

22 R G Albion, *The Rise of New York Port*, New York, 1939, 263.
23 C Cutler, *Queens of the Western Ocean*, Annapolis, 1961, 339.

22

Company offered direct competition to the *Charles Cooper*'s owners as did the Belgian Royal Mail Steam Navigation Company which was founded in 1856 to run services from Antwerp to New York. It had failed by the summer of 1857 which must have been a relief to Hurlbut & Laytin because this offered direct competition for their Antwerp line — the one for which the *Charles Cooper* was intended.[24]

The firm of Hurlbut & Laytin was one of hundreds of family merchant businesses operating in New York. Merchants essentially dealt with importing and exporting goods and often specialised in certain items. They almost inevitably also became involved in related activities, especially shipowning and marine insurance. Elisha Hurlbut started the firm. He was born in 1801 the second son of Samuel Hurlbut, merchant of New London, Connecticut. Elisha almost certainly came to New York in his late teens to serve a commercial apprenticeship in one of the merchant houses. This would have involved learning all the intricacies of book-keeping, manifests, bills of exchange, bills of lading, correspondence and 'outdoor work' such as seeking freights, entering and clearing ships at the Customs House and all the hundreds of tasks of ship husbandry. The only formal training was at 'writing schools' which taught clerks how to write in a copper plate style, usually after work hours.[25] He was twenty-four when he announced his own independent venture, a line of four packets between New York and Mobile, starting with the sailing of the 298 ton schooner *Jane Blossom* on 18th October 1825. The enterprise was successful and expanded, and in the next decade he was joined by three of his brothers. The Mobile service carried both passengers and cargo and in particular brought large quantities of cotton to New York for export to Europe. As Albion noted there was no need for the cotton to go to New York except for its stranglehold over the trade of the Southern states. Its own local exports of flour, meat, wood ash etc. were completely overshadowed by cotton which chiefly went to Liverpool and Le Havre.[26] They ran the Mobile line until 1860 usually with schooners, brigs or barques of under 500 tons. In 1836, they later extended their links to the Florida ports of Apalachicola and Pensacola on the Gulf of Mexico. In 1843, they began a service to New Orleans with larger ships and barques. The largest deployed included the *George Hurlbut* of 1047 tons in 1854 and the *Marianne Netbohn* of 1202 tons in 1856. Quite a few of their vessels (though it is not clear how many were owned and how many chartered for single voyages) seem to have been named after members of the family or business associates.[27] Having established their presence in the coastal packet trade, Hurlbuts then extended their business into the highly competitive Atlantic routes. They started running ships to Le Havre in 1842, but it could not be called a regular packet service until 1845 and even then, no ships were despatched between 1846 and 1848, and in 1851. Cutler lists four sailings for 1854 and notes that sailings were discontinued in 1857, and so this should not be characterised as a packet service because ships were clearly despatched on 'as required' basis and not to a timetable. The New York–Antwerp service was started in 1845 and went on to 1860. It was apparently as irregular as the Le Havre service with no sailings in 1847, 1848, 1852 and 1858 and only one in 1846,1849 and 1853 according to Cutler's records. However, he records the *Charles Cooper*'s first voyage as 1856 instead of 1857 and omits the later voyages altogether which suggests his account may be incomplete.[28]

The Hurlbut's commercial success gained them considerable wealth and Elisha, the founder's share was stated to be $100,000 in 1847. He also had sufficient social standing to be on the board of the New York Hospital and an Incorporator of the Public library by 1850. Two of his brothers in the partnership George and Samuel had died with estates of $50,000 and $30,000.

---

24 N R P Bonsor, *North Atlantic Seaway*, (1st edition) Prescot, 1955, 54-157.

25 R G Albion, 261-2.

26 R G Albion, 99.

27 C Cutler, 397-8, 484,-5, 513, 529.

28 C Cutler, xv, 397-8. Cutler implies in his acknowledgements that he had consulted all the likely American newspapers plus *Lloyd's List* and the Liverpool papers. Suzanne Boorsch used the New York *Journal of Commerce* to establish the *Charles Cooper*'s movements and cargoes.

Above: Some of the dimensions and structure of the **Charles Cooper** *were used for a reconstruction of steerage accommodation for a display about Transatlantic emigration at Merseyside Maritime Museum. The completed bunks and tables give some idea of what the steerage accommodation on the* **Charles Cooper** *must have been like.*

Trustees of NMGM

Above: Individual cabins were cramped with space for no more than luggage and two bunks.

Mark Myers

Right: Steerage passengers in the 'tween decks were crowded into temporary dormitories with eating and social space down the centre of the ship.

Mark Myers

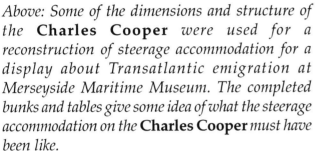

Bottom right: The port side lead outlet pipe from one of the lavatories in the first class accommodation is the sole surviving piece of evidence from the packet voyages. Note the remains of two of the mizzen mast shroud chain plates just below the pipe.

The business continued to be run by Elisha and his remaining brother, John, with the help of their nephew, Peter, the son of their eldest brother, Joseph, a clergyman. Elisha died in 1854. The firm was rebuilt with two new partners from outside the family: William Laytin, a sailmaker and John Ryerson, a shipping merchant. Laytin had been listed at the same address, 84 South Street as Elisha since 1826 and must have been a well known and presumably a trusted supplier; while Ryerson only appeared in the directories in 1854. The new firm was known as Layton, Ryerson & Hurlbut; by 1856 the mysterious Ryerson had moved on. Such was the flexible nature of the small firms that formed the core of New York's shipping business. The partnership then became Laytin & Hurlbut — owners and managers of the *Charles Cooper*. Like many other shipping firms, their offices were in South Street and they loaded and

The port of Antwerp in its mid-19th century hey day. The ship on the right looks as if it could be a packet.

Charles Omell Galleries, London

*R C Leslie's drawing for **Old Sea Ways, Wings and Words**, published in 1890, shows the scene on the deck of an American packet in the 1840s. It is a reminder of just how crowded the main deck would have been with a crowd of emigrants on board. This particular vessel had hen coops on top of a ship's boat to supply eggs for the first class passengers. Doubtless there was a pig or two on board as well.*

discharged their ships from wharf 21 on the East River. All the main packet lines were based on this stretch of the New York waterfront.[29]

New York was the second port after London in the whole world of the 1850s. It handled fifty-two percent of all U.S. imports and exports, and thirty-three percent of the republic's ships were registered there. It was also the main banking and insurance centre. It was also the main port for landing European immigrants. In 1857, 204,000 people arrived there out of a national total of 271,000.[30] Rural poverty (and in the case of the Irish in the late 1840s, outright starvation), persecution or an ambition to be successful in this new land of opportunities were all factors in this huge westward movement. Migrations had risen steadily throughout the first decades of the century and reached boom proportions by the 1840s. Demand for westward passages was of great commercial interest to the New York packet operators. People provided a profitable cargo that could be housed in the tween decks in temporary accommodation.

The *Charles Cooper* loaded at one of the busy South Street wharves. The contemporary photographs show how congested they were with wagons and carts and coastal schooner and canal barges all trying to deliver or collect cargo. The outward cargo consisted of a typical selection of New York exports: 223 bales of cotton, 854 barrels of flour, 25 cases of provisions, 106 cases of pearl ash, 1500 cases of rosin, 50 tons of logwood, 49 hogsheads of tobacco, 150 mahogany logs, 267 tierces of rice, 204 bags of pimentoes, 284,651 pounds of bacon, 7,467 bags of coffee, 9,316 pounds of lard, 25 cases of cod, 2,722 pounds of beeswax, 8400 barrel staves and an unknown amount of nails. There was also accommodation for twelve passengers in permanent cabins in the stern of the ship. These were arranged around the side of a central saloon which served as a dining and social room which was also shared with the ship's officers. It was usually highly decorated with panelling, carving and gilding and ornamental mirrors. There was often one long central table flanked by benches or fixed swivel chairs. The captain usually had separate day and sleeping cabins always on the starboard side. The passenger 'staterooms' were small; six by seven feet was considered spacious. There were usually two bunks about thirty inches wide, one above the other and possibly a washstand. Nevertheless, this was far more pleasant and private than the steerage accommodation in the tween decks. There are no clues in the remains of the *Charles Cooper* about the lay-out of the stern accommodation; but it is highly unlikely that it departed from the typical plan. One fitting does still exist and that is the lead pipe outlet for a water closet on the port side.

The *Charles Cooper* sailed on 11th January 1857 on a passage of some 4279 miles across the Atlantic and up the English Channel to the port of Antwerp. The chances were that it was a stormy passage. Winter in the Atlantic was notorious for gales. The passage commenced and finished at the end of a tow rope. Steam tugs were in regular use and contributed a great deal to the safety of the passage by towing a packet clear the hazards. Their tows also helped to keep the packets to schedule because they did have to wait in port for a favourable wind. A pilot would also be taken. The passage could take up to eight weeks. The first class passengers once they had got over their seasickness probably had a reasonably comfortable time although this to some extent depended on one's fellow passengers. Charles Dickens returning to England on an American packet in June 1842 recorded: *'We breakfasted at eight, lunched at twelve, dined at three and took our tea at half-past seven. We had an abundance of amusements, at dinner was not the least among them: firstly, for its own sake; secondly because of its extraordinary length — its duration, inclusive of all the long pauses between courses, being less than two hours and a half, which was the subject of never failing entertainment'.* He went on to describe all manner of games and music and pleasant socialising and conversation with the wind and the day's passage among the most important topics. The *Charles Cooper* arrived at Antwerp on 2nd March, a passage of just over seven weeks.

Antwerp on the River Scheldt was the main port of Belgium. It had prospered ever since Belgium gained its independence from Spain at the end of the Napoleonic wars. *'Nine tenths*

---

29 Cutler's front endpaper has a map of the port of New York with the wharves named.
30 R G Albion, 267, 418.

of the commerce of Belgium carried by sea centres on Antwerp, which consequently has become a place of great commercial importance. The great article of export are corn especially wheat; flax, butter, cattle, sheep, and pigs; cast and wrought iron; muskets, fowling pieces, and small arms; woollen fabrics; linen ditto; clover and other seeds; coal, spelter, books, etc. The great articles of import are raw cotton, sugar, coffee, and other colonial products; indigo and all sorts of dyewoods; spices, wine, machinery, rice, ashes, fish, oils, etc.'.[31] The tonnage of arriving vessels had doubled between 1850 and 1857 from 205,000 to 420,000 tons.[32] There had been an expansion of the dock system with the opening of the Kattendijk dock in 1853 and the Bonaparte and Willem docks in 1860. It is likely that the *Charles Cooper* as a packet used one of the river quays near the present National Maritime Museum. The port in spite of its growing traffic was not without its problems. It was in direct competition with the Dutch port of Rotterdam whose charges were lower and there was a marked reluctance on the part of the city authorities to invest surplus port revenues on further improvements such as more dock space and cranes.[33] McCulloch listed 22 separate charges for vessels entering and leaving Antwerp including pilotage from Flushing at the mouth of the river, customs dues, harbour dues, quay money, dock pilotage, tonnage dues, hire of cooking houses on the quay because fires were not permitted on board, surveyor's fees, water and ballast charges, etc. The *Charles Cooper* left on April 19th after spending seven weeks discharging and loading. It was a mixed cargo of which many of the barrels and crates were not identified in the notice of arrival at New York on 3rd June 1857. Items that were mentioned included tin, lead, zinc, chloride, 657 kegs of nails, 1348 packages, 869 cases, 1599 boxes and 45 envelopes of glassware (Belgium was a noted glass manufacturer including the finest crystal), wine, and hair (possibly for wigs). All this cargo was stowed in the hold and the tween decks was fitted with temporary bunks to accommodate 287 German emigrants. Twenty-four were farmers and the rest were lumped together as labourers. There were nine first class passengers and a tenth got off at Flushing to take a steamer. Five were merchants, one was a doctor and the other three were not identified. The passage was slow with light winds. There had been one birth on board and icebergs had been spotted on 15th May at latitude 43 15, longitude 49.

The steerage passengers' accommodation was regulated by U.S. Act of 1855. Each passenger was to have fourteen square feet of space, and no ship was to carry more than one passenger per two registered tons. This meant the maximum the *Charles Cooper* was permitted to carry was 488 adults, but the total of 287 for the first voyage was never exceeded in the three other voyages with emigrants. A master was liable to a $50 fine or 6 months imprisonment for every passenger over the legal limit. There was to be a cooking range for the emigrant passengers' exclusive use and a privy for every 100 people. Bunks were to be no more than two high with one for every person measuring six feet by two feet. Specific rations were laid down: twenty pounds of Navy bread (ship's biscuits), fifteen pounds of peas or beans, twenty pounds of potatoes, a pint of vinegar, sixty gallons of fresh water, ten pounds of pork and the same amount of beef both the salted variety. All these were to be rationed to a tenth of the total allocation and issued on a weekly basis. There were also clauses about ventilation. The *Charles Cooper*'s tween deck was eight feet high which must have helped the ventilation. A master could be heavily fined for failing to comply and he could also be fined ten dollars for every passenger over eight years old who died on the voyage.[34] The frequent deaths of very young children was the harsh reality especially for the poor of the 1850s. The *Charles Cooper* proved a healthy ship with only two deaths — an infant and a thirteen year old on the second voyage — out of a total of 822 carried in four voyages. The reconstructed section of an emigrant ship

---

31 J R McCulloch, *A Dictionary practical, theoretical and historical of Commerce and Commercial Navigation*, London, 1859, 44.

32 K Veraght, *The expansion of the port of Antwerp. Cooperation and conflict between the city, the government and the Chamber of Commerce, 1850-1890*, in L M Akveld and J RR Bruijn (editors) *Shipping Companies and Authorities in the 19th and 20th centuries*, Amsterdam, 1986, 125.

33 K Veraght 128-9.

34 T Coleman, *Passage to America*, London, 1972, 292-3.

at Merseyside Maritime Museum, Liverpool is based on dimensions taken from the *Charles Cooper.*

The second voyage was advertised to sail on 1st July, but in fact left on 22nd. This suggests that the owners were having difficulty in finding enough cargo. Captain Lamb moved to the *Marianne Notbohm*, another company ship, and was replaced by captain Rufus Coffin who bought Lamb's share and another sixteenth share from the Laytin & Hurlbut. They also sold a thirty-second share to Samuel Sneden, sailmaker and former partner of Laytin and a sixteenth to Cornelius and Richard Poillon, shipwrights of 44, Water Street. The cargo was similar to the first voyage and included 322 bales of cotton, 50 barrels of potash, 3,268 of rosin, 69 of tobacco, 25 tierces of rice, 25 packages of honey, 715 bags of coffee, 1,155 bundles of hides, logwood, and barrel staves. The return sailing from Antwerp began on 13th October, 1857 and arrived back on November 17th again with a similar cargo to the first voyage, including glassware, lead, wine and a large quantity of unspecified cases and boxes. There were 281 passengers: no first class, a Prussian sailor in steerage (presumably berthed with the crew) and 280 in the tween decks. There were a baker, a blacksmith, a farmer and a cook who were all Americans returning home accompanied by one other person — probably their wives. There were six Belgians, fourteen French, one German, 111 Prussians, 126 Dutch and twenty-three Swiss. Most were craftsmen or farmers and included twenty-six seamstresses. Antwerp had good access to a wide hinterland through a network of waterways and railways. The first of the latter was opened to Cologne as early as 1834.

The third and fourth voyages followed a similar pattern to the first two, both in terms of cargo and passengers. The last was completed in December 1858. Four round trips in two years was what might be expected given the long time spent in port.

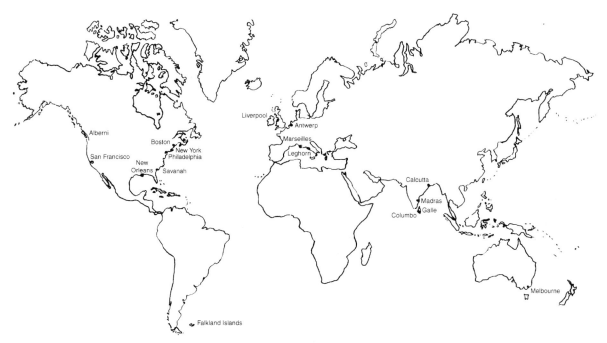

*The **Charles Cooper**'s ports of call on the 'tramping' voyages.*

Liverpool Docks in the 1860s with a North American-built ship alongside the Albert Dock warehouses. The domed building in the background is the Customs House.

Trustees of NMGM

Stanley Dock, Liverpool, where the Charles Cooper berthed, was built in 1848 with warehouses on either side to receive valuable cargoes, such as cotton. It was linked to the Leeds & Liverpool Canal on which barges carried cotton bales to the textile mills of inland Lancashire.

Trustees of NMGM

Chapter 4: WORLD-WIDE VOYAGES

The *Charles Cooper* set sail from New York on the last voyage to Antwerp in April 1859. She had been surveyed in January and she was copper sheathed in Antwerp after discharging a mixed cargo which included cocoa, coffee, potash, honey, rosin, rice, barrel staves, 24 walnut logs,15 casks of copper and 25 barrels of varnish. It is not clear whether this was the first time the ship had been copper sheathed or whether this was a repair or complete renewal. It is likely that the work could be carried out more cheaply at Antwerp than in New York.[35] There are no surviving records of the running costs or the profits.

Some insight into the likely type of out-goings can be gained from the extant accounts of contemporary ships. The China clipper *Houqua*, for example, had the following kinds of expense at New York in 1850: port services, repairs, equipment, stores, crew wages and miscellaneous. Port services included entering the ship at the Customs House, pilotage, towage, discharging and loading costs, dock dues, watchman's wages and cargo surveys. Repairs (and these would vary from voyage to voyage) included joinery, painting, sail and copper repairs. Equipment included cutlery and crockery, cargo books and repairs to the officer's furnishings. Stores covered provisions, water, coal and ship chandlery, and the crew wages in port covered the employment of the master, mate and steward and the shipping of a new crew at the start of the voyage. Finally, miscellaneous covered important items such as insurance, the agent's commission, transport to the ship and advertisements for cargo for the next voyage.[36]

The crew's wages was usually the biggest proportion of a sailing ship's running costs. We do not know how many crew there were on board during the packet ship voyages. An American vessel had to submit a list of the crew at the Customs House before sailing; but none for the *Charles Cooper* seem to have survived. The *Customs Bills of Entry* for Liverpool for 14th July and 29th December 1860 recorded the master and nineteen crew. These probably were: first mate, second mate, boatswain (foreman of the crew), cook, steward (servant to the master and officers), carpenter, sailmaker and twelve seamen. There would have been at least an extra steward and an extra cook on the packet ship voyages to cater for the passengers. There may have been extra crew as well.

The first mate was the ship's executive officer who carried out the master's orders and was responsible for the care of the cargo as well superintending the crew and navigating the ship. He *'ought to be the best workman on board, and to be able to take on the nicest and most difficult jobs, or to show the men how to do them'*.[37] While the first mate had probably gained his master's certificate and had some years of experience as an officer, the second mate was usually a much younger man who had served his apprenticeship and gained his second mate's 'ticket'. He would assist with navigating and cargo duties, but his decision making was circumscribed. Although he was an officer, he was expected to work with the crew on the perpetual round of maintenance and sail handling. The 'craftsmen' the carpenter and the sailmaker (not every vessel carried one of the latter) would have served an apprenticeship ashore at their respective

---

35 This may not be an exact parallel, but the Nova Scotian owned vessel *N B Lewis* was coppered on the Continent (at Le Havre) in 1888 because a cheaper price could be had. See C W Crowell *Nova Scotiaman*, Halifax, 1979, 165.

36 R G Albion, appendix xxi

37 R H Dana, *The Seaman's Friend,* Boston,1857, 149 as quoted by N Dean in *Snow Squall The Last American Clipper Ship,* Gardiner and Bath, Maine, 2001, 92.

craft. The carpenter also had responsibility for the pumps and other mechanical equipment such as winches on board. The cooks were often black, Chinese or disabled seamen. Training was usually on the job but with passengers on board some refinement was necessary. The *Charles Cooper* shipped a Chinese cook on the last voyage who was capable of producing a chicken curry for Mrs. Dean's housewarming party at Stanley.[38] As for the sailors, they were usually young, improvident and tough. They were signed for a voyage and it was not unknown for some to desert on arrival at the outward destination. The chance of a good 'spree' after the hard discipline, harsh conditions, poor food and celibacy of a voyage made them leave behind their sea chests and their accumulated wages in favour of a quick loan and a quick drink from the boarding house keepers who specialised in exploiting sailors. These 'crimps' existed in every major port across the world. While the *Charles Cooper* was at Antwerp between March 12th and May 9th 1858, a US Consul's certificate recorded ten desertions and another ten Americans shipped in their place just before the start of the return voyage.

Once at sea, the two mates picked two watches from the crew. Watches lasted four hours but the time was varied by the insertion of two 2 hour dog watches every afternoon. While at sea there were basic tasks of steering, keeping lookout and tending the sails as required. If there was a major blow then all hands were turned out. The social and command structure was rigid and hierarchical, and hallowed by tradition. All major decisions on navigation, taking in and setting sails were the master's. He had powers in law to punish or fine the crew for a wide range of disciplinary offences. The mates and the boatswain could resort to physical coercion if required and some American ship's officers had a reputation for 'hazing' their crews. The master was a distant figure to the crew who might address them at the start of the voyage and then relay his orders to the crew via the mates. He would never go aloft or engage in manual labour unless he chose to. He was also responsible for the ship's medical chest and treating the crew maladies or injuries. There was no health and safety legislation and going aloft to handle sails on bucking foot-ropes was hazardous, waves breaking on board could sweep men off their feet or overboard and the normal tasks of hauling spars, anchors or whatever could result in sprains, bruises, fractures or hernias. All these and diseases ranging from pneumonia to venereal diseases had to be treated by the master with the help of the *Shipmaster's medical guide*.

Getting back to the voyages: after arrival at Antwerp and the re-coppering, the *Charles Cooper* sailed on July 7th 1859 for Marseilles on the French Mediterranean coast instead of New York. From there she went on to Leghorn in northern Italy (presumably for a return cargo) and arrived back at New York on 4th January 1860: *'Arrived Yesterday ship Chas Cooper, Coffin (master's name), Leghorn Nov. 8 passed the Rock Nov. 18, with mdse (merchandise) to Laytin & Hurlbut. Nov 29 lat. (latitude) 36 23, lon. (longitude) 24 12, saw an object in the water, and steered for it; found it to be a large sky-light. Dec.25 in Gulf Stream, in lat. 37 49, lon. 67 08, passed through a quantity of hogshead headings (lids of barrels). The CC had moderate winds and much calm weather from Gibraltar, till reaching lat. 38 30, lon. 65, since which time had a constant succession of heavy NW and W gales and very severe weather. The thermometer in lat. 37 being as low as 21. Jan 1 & 2, had a severe snow storm from N to NW, everything about the ship and rigging being encased in ice'.*[39] These fragments spotted on the passage to New York were probably the last traces of sailing ships that had gone missing in the winter Atlantic.

The majority, (ten sixteenths) of the shares were put up for sale in February 1860. The advertisement stated that the *Charles Cooper* was three years old, *'built in a most substantial manner'*, has *'a large inventory and well found in every particular'*, *'coppered on her last voyage'*, *'carries a large cargo'* and *'can be seen at Corlear's Hook, where she now lies. For terms apply to CHARLES COOPER at the office of Laytin & Hurlbut, 84 South Street, or to T. Rawson & Co., Bridgeport, Ct'.*[40] The vessel was sold to Alonzo Hamilton, a dry goods merchant from Boston. Hamilton had been born at Waterborough, Maine in 1816. He left home to work in a dry goods store (hard

---

38 Mrs. G M. Dean's diary 4th Oct 1866 photocopy in the Falkland Islands Government Archives (original in private collection).

39 *Journal of Commerce*, New York, 5th January 1860.

ware in Britain) in nearby Saco at the age of sixteen and shortly after opened his own store at
Factory Island with his brother and prospered. By 1849, he was a settled married man with four
children and the Saco Representative in the Maine State Legislature. By 1852 when he moved
to Boston to further his commercial career, he had already become interested in foreign trade
and shipping. He joined the firm of dry goods importers, Turner, Wilson & Co. which he
eventually took over, re-naming it A. Hamilton & Co. All the Bridgeport shareholders had sold
out leaving Laytin & Hurlbut, the Poillions and James Phillips with a sixteenth share each. By
10th March, the *Charles Cooper* was advertised in the *Journal of Commerce* as loading for New
Orleans for the Dispatch Line and sailed round about the third week of March under the
command of George Vaughan Jordan who was forty-nine and came from Saco, Maine. It was
not surprising that Alonzo Hamilton picked someone from his own home town. Once they
sailed a ship's master had to be entrusted with not only the safe navigation of the ships to its
destination but also the transaction of business on arrival. Most shipowners appointed agents
in the ports with which they traded, but this still left the master with many decisions
particularly on return cargoes and repairs.

New Orleans was the second port of the United States and the entrepot for a vast area
thanks to the navigable waters of the Mississippi and Missouri. There were between five and
six thousand boatmen in the port which enjoyed 2,284 river paddle steamer arrivals in 1857.[41]
It was the main exporter of cotton. In 1860, this amounted to $96 million dollars. Much of this
went either to New York or direct to the *Charles Cooper*'s destination, Liverpool. Sailing was
sometime in May 1860 and arrival in the Mersey was 14th July 1860. The cargo consisted of 2,679
bales of cotton, 1,053 sacks of corn (maize) and 3,260 hogshead size barrel staves, and was
discharged at Bramley-Moore Dock, one of a series of new docks opened to the north of the
town in 1848. Eleven other ships, totalling 17,520 tons, arrived from New Orleans on the same
day; they all carried similar cargoes and they were all owned in the United States — such was
the dominance of the Stars and Stripes on the Atlantic. From the Liverpool records it is likely
that the *Charles Cooper* left in ballast for Savannah. A cotton only cargo of 3,177 bales was
loaded there. She set sail on the 17th November and made a reasonable passage of 39 days to
Liverpool arriving on Boxing Day 1860. She was berthed at Stanley Dock. This was a bonded
warehouse dock where cargoes could be directly discharged into large fireproof, secure
warehouses built on the quay. Cotton was by far the most valuable import at Liverpool. It
averaged about £14 million a year and came in at a rate of a 1000 tons a day. The biggest
amount came from the United States.[42]

The *Charles Cooper* loaded a cargo of salt which was a common outward cargo from
Liverpool. Salt was produced from the immense brine deposits in Cheshire around Northwich
and Winsford. The salt was brought down to Liverpool via the river Weaver and the Mersey
estuary in a local type of sailing barge known as a Mersey flat. By this time the threat of civil
war in the United States meant it was imprudent to seek further cargoes in the southern states
which were on the point of seceding from the Union, and so the salt was consigned to Calcutta.
Franklin Jordan who was the nineteen year old master's nephew signed as third officer. He left
a long account of the round voyage.[43] The outward leg was a hard trip of 120 days; the ship was
loaded down to a draft of twenty feet which meant the decks were constantly awash even in
good weather. After starting February, the *Charles Cooper* arrived at the mouth of the Hooghli
in June. Calcutta was the capital of British colonies in India and the main port. Its main exports
were grain, sugar, indigo, silk, cotton and saltpetre and the main imports British manufactures
of all kinds including Lancashire cotton textiles, bullion, metals and alcohol. In 1857–58, some
seventy American (total 51,662 tons) and 315 (total 268,451 tons) British ships entered the port.[44]
Calcutta lay about 100 miles up-river from the mouth of the Hooghli. It was among the most

40   *Journal of Commerce*, New York, 15th February 1860.
41   McCulloch, 884.
42   Braithwaite Poole, *The Commerce of Liverpool*, Liverpool, 1854, 1-3.
43   Alfred T Hill, *Voyages*, New York, 1977, 84-100.

treacherous waterways in the world because of its rapid currents, shifting shoals and quick sands. As a result pilotage was compulsory and Franklin Jordan was struck by the smart naval style of the brig rigged pilot boat. This contrasted with the little cutters and schooners that served the North American ports. The pilot wore a semi-naval uniform and came aboard bringing his Indian servants and his young assistant. He had to be a first class seaman. If a vessel struck a shoal, it would turn broadside to the current and almost certainly be overwhelmed. The trip up to Calcutta took anything between three and seven days. Sometimes the first part could be sailed but steam tugs which were expensive had to be employed for the final stretch. The port was no more than an anchorage served by lighters and discharging and loading was a long-winded process. The *Charles Cooper*'s crew sweltered in hot humid climate; the summer was also the worst time for the spread of disease. The second mate fell sick and had to be discharged and sent home. He died before he reached the Cape of Good Hope. Franklin was promoted to second mate in his place.

After unloading the salt, the ship was dry-docked and re-coppered and in the autumn made a voyage to Columbo and back. The tow lines parted when *Charles Cooper* was being towed out for the voyage, and the first anchor was let go. The strength of the current was so great that it tore out all 540 feet of the cable over the windlass and the cast iron hawse pipe and then snapped the links. The ship went over on its side with the yards touching the water. A second anchor held and the tug was able to re-connect the tow. It was close-run and the day before another ship had touched on the same bank and had been overwhelmed with all hands drowned. The final departure from Columbo was not until 6th April 1862, arriving at Boston after 18,000 miles sailing in September of that year. The cargo included 8,939 bags of linseed, goat skins, hides, gunny cloth (sacking), jute, indigo and 2,555 bags of saltpetre. The latter commodity was of great importance to the Federal war effort because it was a key ingredient of gunpowder. On the passage, there was a mix of weather, with gales off the Cape of Good Hope and fair winds after sighting the island of St. Helena on 6th August. Franklin Jordan's log makes it clear that the ship was almost lost in the worst of the storms: *'July 7 while tacking ship the mainsail was blown to ribbons in a heavy squall … July 11 strong gale from the northwest. Furled mainsail and close-reefed topsails. At midnight took in the foresail and hove to. Gale increasing took in fore and mizzen topsails. Main topsail blew away and fore staysail torn from bolt ropes. Sea ran so high that the main spencer was no use. Lay under bare poles. Storm so terrific it is impossible to keep the ship's reckoning or keep the log. Ship nearly on her beam ends and liable to go down at any moment. All that can be done is to await events. The helm is lashed down and the ship drifting helplessly southward'.* The crew fought back, they managed to set the main upper topsail which was made of new strong canvas on 13th July and the ship continued to *'stagger and reel like a drunken man'* until the storm abated on the 20th. Almost three weeks of gales with everyone drenched to the skin by sea, rain or hail must have sapped the mind and the body and yet this was nothing unusual in a sailing ship passage. Boston must have been a welcome sight.

The ship sailed for Galle in Sri Lanka on 10th November possibly with a cargo of ice. Boston, apart from being the second biggest shipowning port after New York and the biggest fishing port, was the main centre of the ice trade. In the winter, ice was sawn into blocks from frozen rivers and lakes all along the north east coast and transported to the heavily insulated ice houses of Boston. In those pre-refrigerator days, there was a huge demand from hot places across the world where Westerners had settled. Six days before the sailing, the *Charles Cooper*'s shareholders changed. All the old New York and other shareholders sold up and this resulted in Alonzo Hamilton holding eighteen out of the 32 shares, a Cajah Burleigh holding three and Captain George Jordan's wife and his relatives holding the balance. Nothing has been recorded about the voyage. After Galle, the voyage continued (probably in ballast) to Calcutta with a safe arrival sometime in the third week of April 1863. The homeward cargo was similar to the first one: 2837 bags of saltpetre, 9000 bags and 2000 pockets of linseed (the

44 McCulloch 213.

The port of Calcutta not only had a very dangerous approach, but was subject to seasonal cyclones. This picture shows the damage caused by a cyclone in 1863, the year after the **Charles Cooper** *docked there.*

crushed seed yielded an oil for use in paints and varnishes), 12,260 buffalo hides (for the tanners), 41,000 goatskins, 450 bales of jute (for making sacks), 197,500 gunny bags, 50 cases of shellac (a resin produced by tropical ants), lac dye (a red dye from the same insects), 400 cases of castor oil (both lubricant and a medical laxative), 125 bales of coir (coconut fibre) and 71 bundles of unspecified goods. The *Charles Cooper* arrived at Boston on 2nd November 1863 and sailed on 11th February 1864 for Winsor's Regular Line for San Francisco. A local advertisement was not exactly truthful: *'To sail about Jan.25th from India Wharf, the famous clean A1 N.Y. built REAL clipper ship Chas. Cooper!'*

It is fair to assume that the passage round Cape Horn from east to west against the prevailing winds was difficult. The long passage of 166 days suggests this was the case. The fast clippers of the 1850s Gold Rush could make the same passage in under 100 days. Although the peak of the Gold Rush had passed, San Francisco was still partly a shanty town of huts and tents and still with a need to import manufactures, raw materials and fuel from the eastern seaboard industries. The *Charles Cooper*'s cargo reflected these demands and included apples, boots, coal, cordage, pails, cases of oil, pickles and preserves, boxes of soap, steel, pig iron and much more, all valued at $33,033. From San Francisco, Captain Jordan sailed his ship in ballast to load a cargo of timber at Alberni on Vancouver Island for Melbourne. This may suggest that the hull was beginning to deteriorate for timber was often shipped in older vessels that were not dry enough for more valuable cargoes. Perhaps there was no cargo on offer at San Francisco. The hull was certainly staunch enough to carry saltpetre from Calcutta in Spetember. Alberni saw mills advertised that they could supply all kinds of sawn lumber with direct loading which saved 'the tedious navigation of the Fuca Straits'. Its isolated position also meant that there was little risk of the crew deserting. Desertions at all the West Coast ports were a persistent problem for all sailing ship commanders.

The *Charles Cooper* crossed the Pacific between late September 1864 and February 1865 — another long passage. Capture by Confederate commerce raiders was another risk on this type of long cross-ocean passage. However, most, including the infamous *Alabama*, had been eliminated by 1865 and it was only another two months before the surrender of the Confederate armies on 9th April. Melbourne was like San Francisco because it had expanded at a huge rate as a result of the discovery gold in its hinterland in 1851. It was a booming town of 100,000 people. From there, Captain Jordan sailed to Guam on 28th April and then on to Madras and finally, Calcutta again — arriving there on 25th September 1865. She loaded a smaller but similar cargo of saltpetre, castor oil, nux vomica (another medicament), lac dye, shellac and matting. These items were consigned to New York and were safely delivered on April 20th after a long passage. The passage from the mouth of the Hoogli took from 20th of December 1865 to 9th February 1866 — over seven weeks. The winds in the Bay of Bengal were often light and baffling. The Atlantic was reached by 24th February and the Equator crossed again, this time in the Atlantic, a month later. This two year and one month round trip was nothing exceptional for deep sea sailing ships and for any of the crew who managed the full voyage it gave them a great many dollars in their pockets to spend on the New York girls of the famous sea shanty.

A real clipper ship! Nineteenth century advertisements were often flexible with the truth.

The Peabody Essex Museum

Chapter 5: THE DEAN'S HULK

After unloading at New York, Captain Jordan took command of the ***Charles Cooper*** for the last time. He left New York on 20th April 1866, probably in ballast, bound for Philadelphia to pick up a cargo of coal. Philadelphia was the third most important port on the east coast after New York and Boston. It had a large fleet of coastal schooners and had its own line of sailing packets — the Cope Line — which was still managing to keep up its Liverpool service in the face of mounting competition and lack of suitable freights on the outward voyage.[45] It was also linked by a network of canals and railways to coal mines hundreds of miles inland which meant that coal could be exported in large quantities at a competitive price. This consignment was bound for San Francisco. Jordan gave up command after the short passage and handed it to Captain R. W. Dawson. The former was fifty-five years old and perhaps felt worn out by the strains of the recent long voyages. His obituary in the *Biddeford Journal* for 3rd June 1887 (he was 76 when he died) implied that he did not give up the sea and only retired permanently 'a few years ago'. So, there is something a mystery as to why he should give up a ship in which he had a financial stake just before the start of a paying voyage. In the event, he saved himself the trials and humiliation of having to abandon his command.

The ***Charles Cooper*** set sail on 1st June 1866. On 24th July she was reported to be at latitude eleven degrees north, longitude twenty-seven west, north east of Brazil. She was subsequently reported at latitude seven degrees north, twenty-seven degrees, thirty minutes west on 16th August. Progress was often slow when approaching the Equator. Here the strong high pressure Trade Winds die out and are replaced by a region of baffling winds and calms — the Doldrums. The next report was for 25th September, the ***Charles Cooper*** was reported at Stanley in the Falkland Islands leaking. This *Journal of Commerce* report is confirmed by the entry in the Shipping Register at Stanley: 'Charles Cooper, captain W R Dawson, arrived 25 Sept. 1866. From Philadelphia to San Francisco 92 days out, for repairs'.[46] Ten years of voyaging would have weakened the hull and the leak must have been serious for captain Dawson to decide to seek refuge in the Falklands. It was notorious for the high charges for repairs. On the other hand, Stanley was the only place of refuge anywhere near Cape Horn. Unfortunately there is no correspondence in the Government Archives to provide more detail; nor has any evidence of a catastrophic failure of the hull structure been found in the detailed archaeological surveys conducted from 1978 onwards. In fact HM Governor had no powers to regulate the fate of damaged vessels until the Wreck and Salvage Ordinance of 1871.[47] To make things even more mysterious, there is an entry in the Shipping Register on 3rd October which stated that the ship had sailed. So, perhaps there was an attempt to patch the leak and continue the voyage and this then failed causing the master to return to Stanley. Mrs. Dean's diary entry on 4th clearly stated that the Captain Dawson attended her housewarming party that night and that implies the sailing did not take place. This lack of detail stands in contrast to the case of the *Jhelum* of 1871.[48] The latter was a British registered vessel with a British crew and the Governor had to intervene because of the impasse over the state of the hull and the repatriation of the crew. The

---

45 J Killick 'An Early Nineteenth-Century Shipping Line: The Cope Line of Philadelphia and Liverpool Packets,1822-1872', *International Journal of Maritime History*, XII (2000)

46 Falkland Government Archives FIC/AA1

47 I Strange, *The Falkland Islands* 3rd edition, Newton Abbot, 1983,75.

48 M K Stammers & J Kearon, *The Jhelum, A Victorian Merchant Ship*, Far Thrupp, 1993, 42-47.

Governor's letter books are full of the topic including letters from the master begging for help because he and the mate and the steward who had stayed on with him had run out of credit to buy food and a request from the Governor to the Duke of Edinburgh for a survey on the *Jhelum* to be conducted by two of the officers of his ship — HMS *Galatea*.

There was an American Government representative resident in the islands: William Smyley, but he was absent from Stanley on an armed expedition to Patagonia at the time of the *Charles Cooper*'s arrival. That was typical of Smyley, he was an adventurer first and an official second. He was born at Rhode Island in 1792, went to sea as a boy and ended up in the Argentine Navy. His extensive voyages gave him a wonderful knowledge of the intricacies of navigating the coasts of Patagonia and the offshore islands. In the 1820s he is believed to have set himself up at Port San Carlos on East Falkland catching seals for their oil and fur, and wild cattle to sell their beef to passing ships. This was at a time when there was no effective administration in the islands.

This is the point for a brief digression into the history of the colonisation of the islands to explain not only Smyley's position but the development of Stanley as a port of refuge for sailing ships. The first settlements, a French one at Port Louis on East Falkland and a British one at Port Egmont on Saunders Island, were both set up in 1764. Port Louis was handed to the Spanish in 1767. The British were forced out by the Spanish in 1774, but Britain continued to maintain its claim to the islands. Port Louis was abandoned by its Spanish governor in 1806, and the islands became a haven for sealers and whalers, most of them free booting adventurers like William Smyley. In 1820 the former Spanish colony, now the independent republic of Argentina, asserted its rights; but its administrators failed to contain the anarchy. In 1831,the seizure of three American schooners for taking seals illegally brought the sacking of the settlement as a reprisal from the USN *Lexington*. This led to the departure of Louis Vernet, the governor and leaseholder of East Falkland who had done much to encourage settlers. His successor was murdered the following year. The British re-asserted their claim and backed it with separate visits by HMS *Clio* and HMS *Beagle* in 1833. At the same time, Vernet's agent Matthew Brisbane returned from imprisonment on the *Lexington* to try and carry on the settlement. He and three other settlers were murdered by some of their labourers in August 1833. From 1834, there was a naval superintendant backed by an armed naval party to re-assert control. They could not keep up with the cunning Smyley who continued to run an armed schooner and got up to all sorts of illegal activities. When challenged he claimed he was an officer in the US Navy and a government official. He was also a courageous benefactor because he rescued many shipwrecked mariners. His presence had to be accepted as an irritating fact of life by the British.

In 1840, the Colonial Lands and Emigration Commissioners proposed that the islands be colonised and in the following year Lieutenant Richard Moody, aged twenty-eight was appointed as the first civilian governor. He arrived at Port Louis in the January of 1842. He was impressed with the potential of the islands but was hampered by a lack of funds. He did however set up a system of civil government including Legislative and Executive Councils. He also decided after taking the advice of several experienced naval officers to move the seat of government from Port Louis on Berkeley Sound and to Stanley which was named after his boss, Lord Stanley, the Foreign Secretary. It was sited on the inner harbour of Port William. Although the steep-sided hill offered some problems for laying out the new settlement, the harbour offered a much safer anchorage than that at Port Louis.

Settlers were slow in arriving in spite of Samuel Lafone's scheme of 1842 to develop sheep and cattle farming. The most significant group to arrive were a detachment of marines and thirty Chelsea pensioners who were not as ancient as the present day ones and their families. They provided a stable and skilled element in the tiny settlement. Some found pioneering was not to their liking and returned home in 1857. Nevertheless, law and order remained a problem particularly the taking of wild cattle and pigs by American whalers. In 1849, the arrest of the captain of the American schooner *Washington* for killing twenty-two pigs led to a full-blown

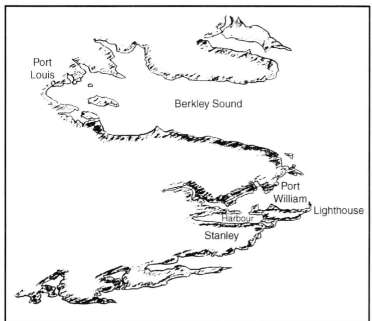

Above: Stanley Harbour in March 1871 on the occasion of the visit of the Duke of Edinburgh, Commander of HMS Galatea. Dean's hulk, the Actaeon, is to the right of centre at the end of his jetty with a two masted schooner alongsides.

Falklands Museum

Left: The approaches to Stanley and its harbour.

Below: In 19th century Stanley, the main port facilities were the jetties which had hulks beached at their outer ends together with the floating storage hulks.

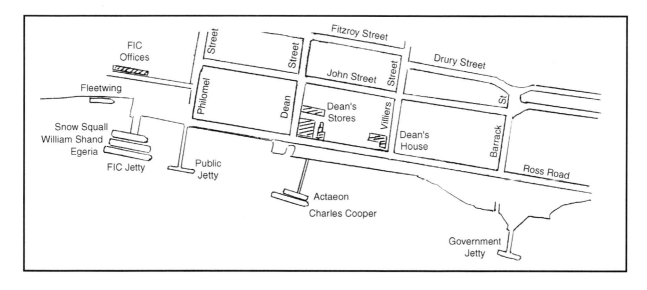

38

This contemporary view of Stanley depicts the Peat Slip of 1878. Dean's premises with the hulk of the **Actaeon** *can be seen on the right.*

Falklands Museum

Stanley in the 1890s from the west. The **Great Britain** *is on the extreme right. The FIC jetty with* **Snow Squall** *and the* **Egeria** *(the latter with a hut on deck) are just off centre. The* **Charles Cooper** *with a barque, possibly the* **Dennis Brundrit**, *alongside can be seen a little way to the left and in the inset.*

Southampton City Museums and Art Galleries

diplomatic incident with the heavily armed US corvette *Germantown* running out its cannon in Stanley and threatening the local administration. Needless to say, Smyley was involved.

Stanley was some 600 hundred miles from Cape Horn and the number of sailing ships that had to pass through its stormy waters increased in the 1840s. First, there was the great boom in guano starting in 1841. This was sea bird droppings that had built up into great mountains on the offshore islands of Peru. It made a valuable fertiliser which became fashionable in European farming. The rapid increase of people living in towns called for an increase in agricultural productivity. Then in 1849 gold was discovered in California and this led to a shipping boom as gold seekers and their provisions were rushed out from the eastern United States. In 1851, gold was found in New South Wales. The gold prospectors travelled by way of the Cape of Good Hope, but the returning ships followed the prevailing wind pattern and sailed home across the Pacific to Cape Horn. Sailing ships had no option but to sail via Cape Horn between the Atlantic and the Pacific. There was no Panama Canal until 1914 and by then there were very few deep sea sailing ships left. Stanley provided a safe anchorage with an entrance that had been surveyed and with a pilot available. It provided provisions, water and a run ashore for exhausted crews battered by the fierce gales of the Horn. It could also carry out repairs; but materials and labour were expensive and there was no dry dock. Work could take months to complete and as a result it developed a bad reputation for exploiting the misfortunes of ships seeking shelter. The incident with the *Washington* and the *Germantown* had made some American vessels wary of calling. For many there was no other option, the next port was Montevideo, another thousand miles to the north. Some ships never made it into Stanley. There were several hundred wrecked on the approaches or outlying islands. Their cargoes were another resource for the locals and sometimes valuable items would be spirited away before the salvage crews could rescue them and bring them to Stanley for auction. Smyley, again, was a noted adept in 'wrecking'. Salvaged cargoes and the cargoes from damaged ships that needed to be lightened before repairs were a storage problem in Stanley. There were only a few small storage buildings ashore. As a result, ships that were too badly damaged to put back to sea were patched up to serve as floating warehouses — hulks.

Apart from Smyley, there were two other trading firms with maritime interests in Stanley: J M Dean and the Falkland Islands Company (FIC to all the locals to this day).John Markham Dean was one of the earliest British settlers and arrived on 17th November 1840 with his wife Charlotte and a young son and a daughter, George and Frances. He was twenty-six and the son of a chemist from Wycombe, Buckinghamshire. He had come to take the job as foreman and clerk, and possibly a junior partner to a Mr Whitington who had set up as a farmer and trader at Port Louis. He soon developed practical experience in the shipping and seal oil business, and was able to cooper his own barrels for shipping seal oil and knew how to dry out wrecked goods to make the most of them. In 1844, the enterprising Dean moved to Stanley and set up on his own account as a general merchant and developed a prosperous business in supplying and repairing ships in salvage and in supplying the local inhabitants. His main store and ship chandlery with a sail maker's loft and a blacksmith's shop was on the site of the present FIC West Store — right opposite the *Charles Cooper*. He also acquired farming interests on Pebble Island in 1862 and Port Stephens in 1870. He and his wife had another five children and three of his sons followed him into the firm.

Dean was already well established by the time the Falkland Islands Company was floated in 1851. It was intended to take over the interests of Samuel Lafone who had been granted sole rights to kill and process the wild cattle in the southern peninsula of East Falkland island under agreements with the Governor signed in 1846 and 1850. Lafone already had an existing cattle processing business in Montevideo which was at a standstill because of war. This and the costs of setting up the Falkland business had been financed by a group of merchants and financiers in the City of London led by Ricketts, Boutcher & Co. The way out of Lafone's difficulties was the formation of a joint stock company to buy out the rights and expand development in the Falklands. The latter included the establishment of sheep farming, a general store at Stanley and a regular postal service to the South American mainland and Europe. The Falkland Islands Company was incorporated in 1851 and received its charter on 1ˢᵗ January 1852. The first years were difficult; the cattle business did not live up to expectations, the sheep business was unsuccessful initially, the postal service made substantial losses, and Deans provided formidable competition on the store and maritime business. It proved to be a great mistake not to have taken Dean into the Company in 1852. The FIC's first manager James Dale wrote to his board in 1853: *'Mr Dean is now considerable in the business of this Colony; he is Lloyd's agent; his capital is estimated at £10,000; his feelings are not I regret to say, of a friendly and pacific character towards the Company, for he looks upon them as his natural enemy; and he is determined to work for far lower profits than hitherto, rather than see business pass him by'.*[49] The FIC's managers were also tied by the financial rules of the company; for example, the store customers were charged ten percent interest on their debts while Dean charged only five and gave unlimited credit, and capital purchases were limited to £300 without the board's approval. This meant it was difficult for the FIC to compete with Dean in buying cargoes from wrecked or damaged ships and the ships themselves. Writing to the board for permission and then receiving their reply took many months and in many instances the board ignored the advice of their managers. The FIC suspected Dean of sharp practice when it came to the disposal of wrecks and in 1862 James Lane complained to Lloyds in London about Dean & Co. There may have been some substance in this. In 1853, Governor Rennie seems to have been aware of cases of collusion between the masters of wrecked or damaged ships and Dean as Lloyd's Agent to sell the vessels or cargoes cheap for their own profit rather than for the insurers. Rennie introduced the Auctioneer's Ordinance which ordained that ships and cargo had to be auctioned off by a licensed auctioneer to counteract such fraudulent deals.[50] In 1854, he received a letter from the Union Insurance Association of North Shields asking him as Governor to arrange an impartial person to survey the barque ***Actaeon*** which had been *'sold and condemned under peculiar circumstances'* which were *'contrary to the warranties of this policy'*. Dean was clearly implicated because he bought the vessel for use as a hulk at his store.[51] The Governor had no powers to follow up this complaint and Dean had acquired a new store and 800 tons of very saleable coal.

In 1864, John Dean left the Falklands to return to England. His eldest son George Markham Dean was left in charge of the business in Stanley and he proved just as adept at business as his father. In September 1866, he took charge of the fate of the ***Charles Cooper***. Mrs. Orissa Dean, George Dean's wife kept a diary at this time and this is the only source of information about the ship at this time apart from the two entries in the Shipping Registers already mentioned. On 4ᵗʰ October she described her house warming dinner at the newly-built Stanley Cottage.[52] The Governor attended; the Vicar, the Reverend Bull was away on Keppel island — 'a good riddance'— and there was a huge menu: turtle soup, curried kidney, roast fowls, roast ducks, boiled leg of mutton, ham and chicken and pie, stewed steak, mushrooms, potatoes, peas, greens, Alma pudding, Marlbro pudding, custards, pink and white blancmange and to drink dessert (wine), port, sherry, champagne, claret and beer.[53] The curry was made by 'Captain Dawson's China boy'. After dinner the men played whist; there was supper at 11.30 and everyone left between two and three in the morning. She added: 'Everyone went well and nothing broken'. The Deans were clearly enjoying a high standard of living in their new house and Pet (Mrs Dean's nickname for her husband) was about to add to the prosperity of the firm

49   FIC Centenary brochure 1951,16.

50   I Strange, 74

51   FIG Archives, Governor's Inward Correspondence, 7ᵗʰ July 1854. The *Actaeon* was a 561 ton barque, built at Miramichi, Canada in 1838 and called at Stanley while on passage from Liverpool to San Francisco, 154 days out, on 27ᵗʰ January 1853.

52   The house still survives on Ross Road, on the Stanley waterfront close to the *Charles Cooper* and is used as the Education Department's offices.

53   According to W Dean's manuscript history of FIC, 113, in 1862 the Rev. Bull apart from his clerical duties ran a savings bank and 'dealt in stores to the extent of selling indecent photographs' Another competitor for FIC.

by acquiring the *Charles Cooper*. Mrs. Dean does not mention the *Charles Cooper* directly but Captain Dawson is mentioned several times and from this we can infer that the business of surveying the ship to establish its seaworthiness, its condemnation and auction must have taken from October until at least the end of December. Captain Dawson came to dinner on 31st October and on 2nd November: *'Pet off at 5 a.m. to inspect a wreck at Port Louis. About 4 p.m. Pet home, as I did not think he would be home again that night, he brought Captain Stratfield and Captain Dawson to dinner. Weather wet.'* Dawson was probably being employed by Dean as Lloyd's Agent to help survey the wreck and its cargo. Visiting or detained masters were often called on to exercise their expertise in this way. On 3rd December: *'Pet went outside to a ship ashore at Port William, came home in the Kate Sargent about 8 o'clock and brought Captain Dawson and the new Captain home to dinner with him'*. Pet was not only late but brought unexpected guests for dinner which must have tried his wife's patience. Mrs Dean also mentioned the *Kate Sargent* which just happened to belong to William Smyley who must have returned from his activities in Patagonia.

He as the US representative would be responsible for the crew. Under a local Ordinance of 1852, American sailors landed in the Falklands were to be treated as foreigners and the US Commercial Agent, i.e. Smyley, was expected to pay a deposit to the Government to indemnify it against them becoming a public liability. US law obliged American ship's masters to take on shipwrecked American sailors at a rate of two per 100 registered tons. In the case of the crew of the American clipper *Snow Squall* condemned at Stanley in 1864, Smyley tried to put most of them on the barque *Orsini* which had come to collect the *Snow Squall*'s cargo. The master sailed before the transfer could take place much to Smyley's irritation.[54] It would be very much in Smyley's interest to get them shipped out either on another American ship or to Montevideo as soon as possible.[55] The master on the other hand had to stay with his ship and its cargo until its disposal had been completed. Captain Dawson came round to the Dean's house on the evening for mince pies. Smyley on the other hand was invited for Christmas dinner which showed how intimate he was with Dean. We hear no more of Captain Dawson after Christmas Day 1866. However the *Boston Shipping List* for 23rd March 1867 reported news sent from Buenos Aires on 25th January that 'Ship Chas Cooper from New York and San Francisco, which was discharging at Stanley, F. I., prior Nov. 6, has been condemned'. This meant that his responsibility to his ship had finished and he could make his way home. It is not clear where the coal was stored, perhaps ashore or perhaps in one of the other floating hulks. It was not sold because the Shipping Register reported the arrival of the American ship *Nor' Wester*, 1,183 tons had arrived on 12th November, 1867 from Montevideo in ballast to call for the coal and deliver it to San Francisco.

Dean's purchased the *Charles Cooper* for use as a floating storage hulk. Its main use was the temporary storage of cargoes from ships under repair. The first step would have been to strip the hull of masts, spars, sails and stores. These could be sold off or saved for re-use on other ships in for repair. The lower masts were retained and probably supported derricks for loading goods into the hold. The loading ports cut through the side of the hull were a later feature. These destroyed the structural integrity of the hull and would have caused sever stress in a floating hulk. They could have only been cut after the ship was beached alongside the *Actaeon* at the West Store. The *Charles Cooper*, the hulk was positioned on a mooring in the middle of the harbour to the west of Dean's stores. An old photograph in the Falklands Museum probably dating from the 1880s shows the hulk almost opposite the Dean's Stanley Cottage. The commercial value of this new store was demonstrated by Dean's competitors at FIC. In 1871, their energetic young manager F E Cobb (who had arrived at Stanley in 1867) wrote to his board: *'I need not say more than I have done about the want of a hulk. I am paying Dean £3 6s 8d*

---

54 N Dean 194-5.

55 It seems likely that Smyley was absent from Stanley because he wrote to US Secretary of State on 2nd August 1866 stating that he was going to try and reinforce the US Schooner *Totton*'s armed expedition to San Pinau in Patagonia. Boorsch, 22.

per day for the **Charles Cooper** *having to engage her for the Italian who would have used our hulk if had one'.*[56] Cobb had pointed out to the board in 1868 that he only had the *Margaret* and the *William Shand* as storage hulks and he needed a sound hull to compete with Dean. Both his hulks leaked and were only fit for coal storage. He went on to write that 'Dean has such an advantage over the Company that I do not believe he would allow another [ship] to go at auction under £1000 to £1200.[57] That same year Cobb gained the Lloyd's agency from Dean but it seemed to cause more trouble than it was worth. Dean continued to compete with FIC just as hard as before. He was the main supplier of steam coal and provisions to visiting naval vessels and he handled some at least of the Governor's stores. In June 1868, after Smyley's death from cholera at Montevideo, he got himself appointed as US Vice Commercial Agent. In 1869, he was able to buy Pebble Island for only £400. This saga of George Dean beating Cobb and the FIC at every turn continued right up to his death in 1888. Three later examples of his astuteness were the purchase of the barque *Dennis Brundrit* for a £355 when it was worth £7000 and the purchase of the dismasted ship *Sussex* and the cargo of coal for £3000 when it was worth £10,000. In 1882, he bought a small coasting steamer, the *Ranee* for work around the Camp settlements which took work away from the Company's schooners.[58]

George Dean died on 1st April 1881 aged only fifty-one and was buried in an impressive pink marble tomb — the biggest in the cemetery at Stanley. He had been not only Vice Consul for the USA, but also Consul to Denmark, Sweden and Norway, a Justice of the Peace and a member of the Legislative Council. There was no one of the Dean family who wanted to continue the business in Stanley and it was offered to the FIC. Terms were agreed in October 1888 and they bought their rival for £27,225 plus a valuation of the book debts and stores.[59] It included all the buildings and facilities but not the land in Camp. Cobb found that the *Charles Cooper* was not the valuable asset that it was in 1871: '*Charles Cooper, an old one, the decks are bad and neglected down below'.* He did have a use for her: '*The jetty [Dean's] is good, far better than our own though both want lengthening. The* **Charles Cooper** *and the* **Capricorn** *will do for this purpose'.*[60] It is not clear exactly when the *Charles Cooper* was beached. On 12th August 1892 A.E. Baillon (Cobb's successor) reported the arrival of the *Dennis Brundrit* from England bringing much-needed supplies of house coal: '*The* **Dennis Brundrit** *arrived on 6th, 82 days from the Downs, all in good order and has come alongside the* **Charles Cooper** *this morning'.*[61] This probably means that the *Charles Cooper* was still afloat. Given the shallow depth alongside the hulk today, it seems unlikely the fully-loaded *Dennis Brundrit* would have been able to berth alongside which must have been at least twelve to fourteen feet. Baillon may have beached the *Charles Cooper* in 1895 when the FIC's Depreciation Book noted the expenditure of £220 6s 6d for repairs to the West Jetty, sea wall and the ship. Perhaps this was because his dispute with the Governor and the Harbour Master about the hulks at the FIC's East Jetty had been resolved. There were two hulks beached at the end of this jetty: the *William Shand* and the American clipper *Snow Squall* which had been condemned in 1864. It appeared that the FIC had not sought permission from the Harbour Master as the Government representative to place these hulks on the foreshore. He suspected that the Governor was behind what he saw as an unnecessary persecution of the company and asked the board to protest to the Colonial Secretary and [I] '*trust that you may be more successful in defeating his nefarious schemes'.*[62] In 1893 the Colonial Office did take a view which was more lenient than the Governor's. It was left to

56 FIC Archives, Colonial Manager's Despatches 23rd September 1871. The Italian was the barque *Anna Paradi* had arrived leaking and damaged.

57 FIC Archives, Colonial Manager's Despatches 7th April 1868 'No amount of caulking can repair the *Margaret* now' and the *William Shand* was leaking below the waterline

58 W Dean's manuscript history of FIC, shipping further notes, unnumbered appendix.

59 FIC Board Minutes 15th October 1888.

60 FIC Colonial Manager's Despatches 15th January 1889.

61 FIC Colonial Manager's Despatches 12th August 1892.

62 FIC Archives, Colonial Manager's Despatches 17th August 1892.

Right: The **Charles Cooper**'s 'tween decks were used to store building materials. Note the painted name on the deck beam which is dated 30th May 1955, and there were still many drain pipes on board at the time this photograph was taken in 1966.

John Smith, Stanley

Below: There were still a few broken drain pipes and soil traps on baord in 1978.

A similar view taken in 1998 shows the extent of the deterioration with all the planking, frames and ceiling washed away on the wind and water line.

Baillon's successor W. A. Harding who took over as FIC 's Colonial Manager in 1898 to improve the usefulness of the **Charles Cooper**. The storage value of a hulk depended largely on it being dry. The decks on the **Charles Cooper** still show evidence of being caulked and flooded with pitch to try keep them tight. Harding who was probably the most able of all the FIC's managers came up with an ingenious and frugal solution. *'A large quantity of roofing iron ex **Samoa** is damaged by salt and cannot be sold as sound. It appears to me that rather than sell it at about £8 per ton, we could put it to a very profitable use by roofing over the whole of the **Charles Cooper**. At present the hulk is useless for storage purposes, whereas with a roof over the upper deck, we should have excellent storage accommodation'.*[63] The roof work was completed by April 1901 at a cost of £361, £90 above the estimate and this was because the good corrugated iron at £16 a ton from the *Samoa* was used and a higher pitched roof was built so that the upper deck could be used for timber storage. The cost was about the same as sheathing the *Egeria's* deck which was unsatisfactory because it leaked causing the loss of £20 of salt.[64] The new dry storage was put to immediate use because it meant that goods did not have to be stored in the lower hold of the *Egeria*. It took a lot of labour to handle goods in and out of this space. It also meant that the **Great Britain**, which was another difficult space to work mixed stores, could be devoted to wool bales. There was also a possibility of warehousing naval stores because of a threat from the Uruguayan government to impose an import duty on them.[65] A year to complete a roof may seem rather slow but there was never enough labour for all the FIC's jobs and as Baillon pointed out in 1895 not all its employees worked flat out: *'Most of our men have had constant work for far too long and [it is] hopeless to expect improvement. Biggs [foreman shipwright] has three sons working for him and Johnson's three or four are faithful to their foreman and never pass a public house without patronising the bar'.*[66]

The **Charles Cooper** continued to perform a valuable storage job role with little mention in the FIC's records. The jetty out from the shore crossed the remains of the decayed **Actaeon** and was extended through the centre of the ship to form a loading port on the outer side of the hull. Lighters and schooner could berth alongside to discharge cargoes. There was also a narrow gauge tramway for moving goods with hand pushed trucks. The Depreciation Book noted that repairs estimated at £100 were cancelled in 1910. The jetty was completely rebuilt using reinforced concrete piles and the spars from the French four-masted barque **Fennia**. It is not clear when this work was carried out. It must have been after the *Fennia's* arrival and condemnation in 1927, although the FIC completely rebuilt the East Jetty in 1929 with increased warehouse space for most dry goods imported from England. The **Charles Cooper's** storage was mainly for coal in the forward tween decks and building materials and sanitary ware in the after part. The original roof was still in place after the Second World War and was replaced by a smart new aluminium one sometime probably in the 1950s. In the 1960s, the hulk was not much used and eventually it was decided to abandon it and dismantle most of the jetty to avoid paying rates on it.[67] In 1968, when the hulk was sold to the South Street Seaport Museum for $5000, it was still valued at £487 8s — the price paid to Deans in 1889!

---

63 FIC Archives Colonial Manager's Despatches 2nd November 1900.
64 FIC Archives Colonial Manager's Despatches 29th April 1901. The *Egeria* was a 1066 ton Canadian-built barque of 1859, condemned in 1872 and bought by FIC as a floating hulk and eventually beached outside the *William Shand* at the East Jetty.
65 FIC Archives, Colonial Manager's Despatches 5th March 1901
66 FIC Archives, Colonial Manager's Despatches 16th October 1895.
67 I am grateful to John Smith, Terry Spruce and Gerald Roberts for filling in this gap in the records from their memories of this later period.

Chapter 6: A PIECE OF MARITIME HERITAGE

The **Charles Cooper** was bought by South Street Seaport Museum with a donation of $5000 from the New York *Journal of Commerce* — the shipping newspaper that had reported the ship's arrivals and departures. It was declared to be: *'the most important American sailing ship surviving from the 19ᵗʰ century'* and that *'It is hoped that her remarkably well-preserved wooden hull can someday be placed on exhibit in the port of New York'*.[68] But why should New York want to preserve a large deteriorating wooden sailing ship hulk ?

Any of the **Charles Cooper**'s owners or any other 19ᵗʰ century shipowner would have derided the notion of preserving a ship beyond the time of its commercial use. They took great pride in the appearance of their ships. They memorialised them through commissioning paintings and models; but they had no regrets or sentiments about having them broken up. The idea of preserving such large man-made objects was a late 20ᵗʰ century phenomenon. Common sense would suggest that the salvage of objects such as an incomplete, structurally unsound, 165 foot wooden hull abandoned in a hostile environment in a remote port was not good idea. The reasons for the rise in ship preservation of sailing ships go back to first part of the 20ᵗʰ century. Even before the First World War it was clear that the day of the commercial sailing ship and fishing boat was over. War losses, scrappings, wrecks and the lack of replacements reduced the fleet still further. It was seen as the end of an era and that a singular way of life accompanied by a range of complex seafaring skills was about to disappear for ever. This was regretted by merchant marine officers who had trained as apprentices in sail and also by outsiders attracted by its adventure and its powerful sense of nostalgia. Many of the latter took the singular step of leaving comfortable homes and jobs to make one voyage in a deep sea square rigger before it was too late. One of the pioneers was Basil Lubbock (1876-1942), an Old Etonian who liked adventures. In 1902, his book *Round the Horn before the Mast* was published and went through four separate printings and editions up to 1911. It was his autobiographical account of a voyage back to England in the forecastle of a four masted barque from gold prospecting in the Klondyke. Between 1914 and 1937 he wrote a series of influential books on deep sea sailing ships which were largely drawn from the reminiscences of old masters and were full of nostalgia for iron men and beautiful ships. They are still in print. Public interest was heightened by stories and pictures about the last sailing ships in newspapers and the rise of specialist 'shiplover' magazines such as *Sea Breezes*. Alan Villiers (1903-1982) was an Australian journalist turned 'sea dog' who wrote many hooks based on his experiences under sail and also tried to keep the experience ,the values and skills of working in square riggers by running his own training ship, the *Joseph Conrad* between 1934 and 1936. After the Second World War he gained further fame and wrote more books by commanding a number of replica ships such as the *Mayflower 2*. His *Jospeh Conrad* venture exemplified the approach to preservation which valued the square rigger as a teaching tool for life particularly a professional life at sea.[69]

Scandanavians continued to serve apprenticeships in the last commercial deep sea sailing ships, most notably those owned by journalist turned sea dog Gustav Erikson who tried to keep the experience. Training under sail was also valued by some merchant marine academies

[68] *Seaport* Summer 1983, 26.
[69] Villiers did also support museum ship preservation certainly in later life. For example , he supported the campaign to save the *Wavertree* by travelling to New York at his own expense to give two fundraising lectures.

and navies which had the resources to build and run specialist sail training ships. This movement has grown and prospered since the 1950s and is sometimes seen as the cure-all for the ills of disaffected youth.

The other thread that emerged from this growing belief in the need to preserve the past sailing ship era was the movement to save the actual ships or at least sections of them. In the United States, the single most important figure was Karl Kortum. He had been brought up on a farm in California; in 1941, he had the chance to sail before the mast on the barque *Kaiulani* carrying timber from San Francisco to Durban. In 1951, he established a maritime museum at San Francisco. The collections included sections from historic ships and in 1955 he was able to acquire the three masted ship *Balclutha*, an iron vessel of 1862 tons built on the Clyde in 1886. After serving in the seasonal trade of the Alaska salmon canneries, it had been converted to 'a waterfront attraction' in the 1930s. Kortum proceeded to add more large vessels to the Museum's collection — an inheritance which has caused some headaches for his successors. He also began a mission to seek other sailing ships that could be saved for posterity. In 1966, he travelled to Argentina and the Falklands on his quest. Awareness of the unique collection of sailing ship hulks that existed in Stanley harbour had been growing. Even in 1908, George Dunbar a first voyage apprentice on the Liverpool barque *Gladova* wrote home: *'The harbour is full of hulks. There is a sailing ship called **Glen Gowan** 89 days off the stocks but in here afire. There is also the old **Great Britain** one of the Cunard liners* [wrong]. *There is also an old sailing ship one hundred years old* [probably the *Margaret*]*'*.[70] In 1917, the Cathedral Press run by the Rev C MacDonald at Stanley published a small guide to the islands which included a description and list of the hulks including the *Charles Cooper*. In 1933 volume sixteen of the *Sea Breezes* magazine published a list of hulks submitted by Karl Lellman — a Stanley resident. Kortum's reconnaissance was a success. He re-discovered the British ship *Wavertree* as a sand barge in the back channels of Buenos Aires and persuaded the infant South Street Seaport Museum in New York to acquire it for restoration. He also believed that Brunel's revolutionary screw steamer the *Great Britain* of 1843 could be salvaged from Sparrow Cove. Afterwards he visited Frank Carr the Director of the National Maritime Museum, Greenwich to press for a preservation campaign and applied some pressure by assuring Carr that if Britain was not prepared to save its maritime heritage then San Francisco would.[71] Kortum's intervention proved timely because others in Britain were thinking along the same lines and in 1970 the *Great Britain* was successfully salvaged and brought back for preservation in her building dock at Bristol.

He played the role of catalyst in relation to other hulks he had surveyed in the Falklands. These included the floating hulk *Fennia*, the *Vicar of Bray* a wooden British barque that had berthed at San Francisco during the Gold Rush, the *Jhelum* and the *Charles Cooper*. There seemed to be little prospect for the long term preservation of these historic ships where they lay and this was reinforced by the likelihood that the British might give up the islands at some point. On the *Jhelum* for example, he wrote in 1972: *'Jhelum, which I visited in 1966 would make a splendid display. In my opinion she shouldd be cut off at the waterline and displayed inside a building, probably with simulated masts in place. … Jhelum is a two part display. The forward half of the vessel is a silvered skeleton, a thing of beauty. By being reduced by the elements (largely) to a skeleton, it conveys the way the vessel is put together'*.[72]

Kortum was blessed with great imagination and great energy. At around the same time as his Falklands expedition he was also involved in the campaign to save his old ship, the *Kaiulani* which was languishing as a barge in the Phillipines. The campaign failed although he was able to secure a section of bow and stern for his own museum; but the National Maritime Historic Society grew out of that and it in turn played a leading role in saving the last remaining streets and wharves from New York's sailing ship era — South Street.

[70] Merseyside Maritime Museum Archives DX/SAS
[71] P Stanford's preface to N Brouwer's *International Register of Historic Ships* 2nd edition, Oswestry,1993, 9.
[72] K Kortum letter to M K Stammers 31st October 1972.

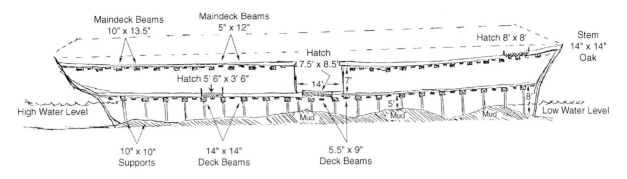

Maindeck Beams 10" x 13.5"   Maindeck Beams 5" x 12"   Hatch 8' x 8'   Stem 14" x 14" Oak

Hatch 7.5' x 8.5'

Hatch 5' 6" x 3' 6"   14'   7'

High Water Level   Mud   Mud   Mud   Low Water Level   5'   8'

10" x 10" Supports   14" x 14" Deck Beams   5.5" x 9" Deck Beams

John Smith made the first detailed survey of the hulk in 1966. The hull was embedded in the mud, but it still seemed to be a candidate for salvage.

John Smith, Stanley

*The **Charles Cooper** from Victory Green in 1978 still looks intact and in good condition.*

Above: A view of the starboard side in the same year shows damage to the frames.

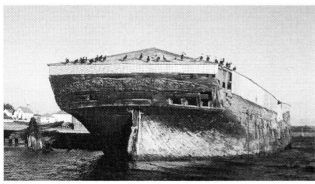

Left: A view of the stern, also from 1978.

Left: Hilton Matthews taking measurements on the starboard side in 1978.

Below: The pieces of the stern carving were moved ashore on the FIC's tug. Eric Berryman and Norman Brouwer carry a section down the Public Jetty with a local assistant.

Left: Waiting for the Museum to open, Peter Throckmorton discusses the stern carving with Zak Hirtle, another local helper.

Right: The process of deterioration is clear in this photograph of the starboard quarter. The planking at wind and water line has been washed off, which has exposed the frames and ceiling. By 1990, only a few weakened frames were left and the upper part of the hull was being supported by the ceiling and the strength of the deck beams.

Left: The port side was not so exposed to the force of the wind and waves. Nevertheless, this has lost planking on the wind and water line. Plant life and nesting birds had caused damage and rot in the planking above the water.

He had a vision that was shared by the South Street Seaport Museum's first director, Peter Stanford of seeing square riggers with their bowsprits projecting out over the Street as they did in the 19th century. The ownership of the *Charles Cooper* had been secured and in 1970 the *Wavertree* was towed back for restoration .

The first detailed survey was undertaken by John Smith in 1970. At the time John worked for FIC, but in his spare time he took a great interest in the history of the islands, especially the hulks. He also ran a small museum with Joan Spruce at one end of the FIC offices in Crozier Place. Among the treasures packed into this small room were the trail boards which had been found floating in the harbour. John's report was thorough, detailed and tended to rule out any easy cheap salvage. Much of the outer planking on both sides was rotten and entirely missing amidships. This meant that the frames were vulnerable to wave action and they in turn would eventually be weakened and collapse. The main longitudinal timbers had also been cut away at that point leaving the hull structurally weak. It was still possible to walk in the hold at low tide.

He thought the cost of patching and strengthening for refloating would cost a tremendous amount of money. He had consulted Leslie O'Neill, the salvage expert on the *Great Britain* who thought it could be floated long enough to get it on to a pontoon. John added; *'I think he was looking at the idea from the view of a large salvage operator where everything is possible if there is enough money'*. He added: *'She could be cut up into bits and shipped away then re-assembled like a giant jig-saw puzzle'*. This was the technique used for the salvage of sections of the remains of the *St Mary* in 1978 and the *Snow Squall* in 1987. At this time South Street Seaport were still undecided about moving the *Charles Cooper* back to New York because of the different environment. It was always thought that the chilly waters of the Falklands had helped preserve the timbers. John thought that if the hold could be filled with stone and concrete it would make a stable base for preserving the upper works in situ. He felt that this *'could make her one of the most unique maritime museums in the world'*. He pointed out that tourists were likely to increase with calls from cruise liners and the proposed building of an airport. What a pity it did not happen. The report in hindsight also hinted at a tension between the views of the local people who had grown up with the hulks and the endeavours of the maritime historians trying to save ships and take them away from the islands for restoration. This tension was increased after the *Fennia,* the last floating hulk and a prominent landmark, was towed to Montevideo en route for preservation in California about 1976. The salvors ran out of money and the abandoned vessel was eventually broken up.

South Street Seaport mounted three expeditions to the Falklands in 1976, 1978 and 1981. The 1976 party consisted of Norman Brouwer, the archivist and librarian at South Street, Hilton Matthews, an English shipwright who had been working on the restoration of *Wavertree* and Peter Throckmorton. Peter was by then Curator-at-Large for the National Maritime Historical Society; he has had a varied career including naval service and university research jobs. *'He was not the type to stay in any niche; restless and exploratory, without formal university studies, he was destined to carve out new paths in the research of ancient shipwrecks'.*[73] He became a pioneer of underwater archaeology and was one of the two leaders for the first systematic underwater excavation at Cape Gelydonia in 1960. He had run his own schooner, the *Stormie Seas*, for charter and diving work in the Mediterranean. He, like Kortum, had a crusading zeal to save historic ships and wrecks which bordered on the mystical: *'Why historical preservation ? One cogent reason for these things is shortest expressed in the almost forgotten language of the earliest Polynesian voyagers, Reo Tumu (root language). It's mana… best but insufficiently translated as spiritual force… The Mana of physical objects fills a deep need in mankind. What these objects prove is that mana which is abstract can be physical. Historical objects in a museum, relics in a reliquary, demonstrate to the laos that we, the priests, or scholars or the Most Modern of high priests, the scientists, know what we are talking about… I have been a historical preservationist all my life first because I feel the mana in historic objects, which is either a result of being partially educated by clerics, or perhaps just through being North American, but mainly, because it seems to me that the public has got to be convinced*

---

73   H Kritzas 'Peter Throckmorton, an Odysseus of the Deep', *Enaaia supplement 2,* Athens 1991,15.

that spending money on ancient ships is a right thing to do'.[74] Throckmorton was also prepared to put his own money on the line. When he spotted the little iron barque *Elissa* (then a motor ship) laid up and ready for the Greek breaker's yard, he raised the funds to save it and was eventually able to sell it to the Galveston Historical Society for preservation. He also had in his own words *'a genius for alienating bureaucrats'* which made him enemies in Greece and obliged him to move back to the family farm in Maine in 1976.

Brouwer's, Matthews' and Throckmorton's visit in 1976 was to reconnoitre for a larger expedition. They identified the detailed recording of the *Charles Cooper* as the main priority with smaller recording projects on the clipper *Snow Squall* at FIC's east jetty. The plan was to try and combine the full scale recording of the *Charles Cooper* and on the Downeaster *St Mary* at Pleasant Roads. There was also to be if possible a dive on the iron four masted barque *John R Kelley* in Port Williams and an inspection of the wreck of the packet ship *Helen A Miller* at Port San Carlos. with field work on the wrecks of other American built ships in the islands. An application for funding to the Foundation for the Arts and Humanities was successful and the expedition was to take place in January 1978. The original trio were supplemented by Dr Eric Berryman of the University of New Mexico and a naval reservist, Mrs Avery Stone, a volunteer diver, and the author. Later on four more volunteers arrived from Earthwatch as well as the crew of three from the visiting yacht *Jennie Wren*. The original objective of recording had been widened to the recovery of forty foot of the *St Mary*. This was a prime example of the last big wooden square rigged sailing ships built in the USA. One of Peter Throckmorton's lectures about his 1976 visit inspired the Maine State Museum to help fund the recovery of a section of the tween decks. Without dwelling on the detail, the recovery was successful in spite of the difficulties of dismantling and transport on a remote beach. It forms a very successful exhibit in the Maine State Museum in Augusta. This was very much thanks to Throckmorton's 'can do' approach and Berryman's organisational skills and naval contacts. On top of this, Throckmorton had arranged to bring a team of film makers down to make 'Ghosts of Cape Horn'. This widening of the objectives did not so much divert energy away from the *Charles Cooper* work but did create tensions. At one point towards the end Throckmorton wrote that one of his colleagues exuded *'a hatred vibe that would curl the bark off a tree'.*[75] He did not get on all that well with the locals. He was frustrated by what he saw as their dog in manager attitude to the wrecks and they perceived him as a piratical looter. Having said that, the work on board went well. A series of detailed measurements and photographs of the hull structure and fittings were secured. These included a series of cross sections which involved the co-ordination of measurements across the hull inside, measurements down to the waterline from a ladder placed in a boat or on a pontoon and measurements underwater to the turn of bilge. The stern carving which was threatening to fall into the water was carefully dismantled, cleaned and a silicone rubber mould made of it. The original was to be kept by the Falklands Museum while the moulds were sent back to the United States to make a full scale replica. The survey work also showed how the structure was deteriorating. The stanchions and the framing in the hold were becoming badly eroded and the upper tween deck structure was sagging especially at the midships loading port. New shores were installed to try and arrest the process. In 1981, Norman Brouwer went to Stanley again to install more shores. By then, the imaginative vision of the South Seaport's founders had been submerged by the reality of an independent body having to pay its way and stay in existence in a prime area of real estate. Any plans for the entire recovery of the ship were on hold and became less and less likely as the deterioration continued.

The 1978 expedition besides its information gathering and conservation work had other positive outcome. It created more interest in the Falkland wrecks. There were detailed surveys carried out on the *Vicar of Bray, Jhelum, Lady Elizabeth* and *Egeria*. There was also some conservation carried out on the *Jhelum* and the bow section of the *Snow Squall* was recovered

---

[74] Peter Throckmorton to M K Stammers 15th March 1978 from Stanley.
[75] *ditto*

Right: By 1998, the starboard 'tween decks werer always under water at high tide.

Left: The port bow in 1990 was beginning to loose its planking. The square was a timber port which was probably cut for loading the cargo of timber at Alberni in 1864.

Above: This composite photograph from 1990 shows the extent of the deterioration and the deformation of the hull as the starboard side slowly collapses.

Left: The collapsing process even caused the massive transom beam to crack. Such was the weight involved.

Right:The starboard side has collapsed at wind and water level which meant the whole weight of the upper works has hanging from the deck beams. This caused the deck beams to crack and in some cases break completely.

Above: The smaller gribble were at work on the interior deck planks. This is the forward 'tween deck in 1998 with only the iron fastenings remaining.

The boring activities of the Teredo have accelerated the deterioration. This is a section of one of the piles from the Public Jetty that has been saved by David Eynon. It shows how the large holes running down the grain of the timber have weakened it. Note that it was sheathed with copper sheet. This protection clearly did not work.

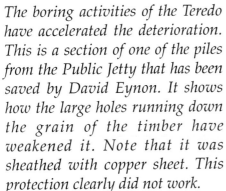

Above right: By 2002, the whole starboard side had collapsed and the roof removed.

Above: The stern was almost under water and the starboard side is on the point of breaking away.

Right: On the port side as a result of the collapse, there was massive distrotion. The huge waterways, with their fine moulding, have been forced into a hump amidships.

and taken back to Maine for preservation.[76] It also created a greater awareness of the islands' maritime heritage among the islanders and support organisations such as the Falklands Islands Foundation. In 1977, it also resulted in local legislation to protect the maritime heritage above and below the water. The next threat came from an unexpected source. The Falklands were invaded by Argentine troops on 2nd April 1982 and when it became clear that the British would contest their occupation Stanley became an armed camp. Attack from the air was always a threat, but on the ground Argentine conscripts were foraging for fuel and it was only a matter of time before they started chopping pieces of timber from the hulks to keep themselves warm. John Smith used his previous contacts with the Argentine military to ask for the local heritage to be protected: *'I put it to them that if the Islands were theirs, then all the history and heritage were theirs also, and should be looked after accordingly. This worked… Things went so agreeably that it was possible to point out the importance of the shipwrecks and hulks in the harbour. A permanent reminder of the maritime heritage of the Islands, their importance was now being recognized on a world–wide scale… It was of the utmost urgency that the troops did not saw them up for firewood or damage them in any way'.*

He was supported by Captain Hussey, the Argentine Navy representative, and the hulks were placed out of bounds and Smith given a special pass to check on them. The pass worked and on 29th April he was allowed to row out to the *Charles Cooper* in spite of the fact that it was surrounded by troops. The hulk of the Welsh brig *Fleetwing* was the only one to be damaged, losing some stern timbers.[77] After the War, most the attention was on putting the town back to rights. The *Charles Cooper* survived but was still deteriorating and the process was probably speeded up by the wash from a large number of ships using the harbour. The value of making a detailed record when it is not possible to recover the actual structure was demonstrated in 1986 when Merseyside Maritime Museum opened its *Emigrants to a New World* gallery. The main exhibit was a midships section of the tween deck of a Transatlantic emigrant ship of the 1850s. It was properly constructed in timber and most of its dimensions were modelled on those of the *Charles Cooper*. The next detailed survey was carried out by John Kearon and Jim Forrester, ship conservators at Merseyside Maritime Museum in December 1987. They were part of the *Jhelum* recording team but were able to spend time on a survey and in fastening down the roof which was beginning to fly apart. Their report pointed out that sixty feet of the starboard planking to a height of four feet above the high watermark had disappeared and that the hulk relied on its internal timbers. These were under attack and it was only a matter of time before the whole of the outer starboard side was suspended in mid-air without any support on the inter-tidal zone. This in turn would lead to the breaking of the main deck beams and the collapse of the tween deck stanchions. There were patches of rot inside caused by bird guano and the rapidly developing plant life. There were eight large holes in the roof which allowed the birds access. The harbour authorities were also concerned about the risk of large chunks of timber being prised away and presenting a dangerous floating hazard to the fast launches. Subsequently old trawl nets were used to prevent birds getting in and loose timbers escaping. This was partially successful. It drew protests from the bird supporters because a number of steamer ducks got trapped and died and eventually the polypropylene netting was broken down by the strength of the ultra violet light. Merseyside Maritime Museum's field trips in 1990 provided further evidence of decline. The main deck and the transom beams were beginning to crack and the stern post had been eroded to about fifty percent of it original dimensions. South Street Seaport Museum were still the owners. But given their problems at home there was no longer any possibility of action in the Falklands and in 1991 they handed

[76]   *Vicar of Bray,* unpublished feasability study for moving to San Francisco 1978; *Jhelum,* Stammers & Kearon, see note 48; *Lady Elizabeth,* F Yalouris and F Feyling, 'Report on the British barque *Lady Elizabeth'* in *The Falkland Islands Journal,* 1986, 22-36; *Egeria* E Lawson 'The *Egeria* story' in the *Falkland Island Journal,* 1986 15-19 and forthcoming book; *Snow Squall,* D C Switzer 'Epilogue : back to the Falklands' in N Dean, *Snow Squall, The Last American Clipper Ship,* Maine, 2001, 212-269.

[77]   J Smith, *74 Days An Islander's Diary of the Falklands Occupation,* London, 1984, 91, 106, 221.

ownership to the Falklands Islands Museum and National Trust. There were attempts to mount expeditions from the United States. The Institute of Nautical Archaeology based in Texas considered a project. Nicholas Dean and the *Snow Squall* team offered help to continue recording and develop a stabilisation plan and if the worst were to happen selective salvage of key sections. But there were no funds. The veteran Karl Kortum proposed the total removal of the whole tween deck section back to the United States. He was however out of touch with the prevailing sentiment of the islanders. Nicholas Dean pointed out to him that *'more or less total removal of a long time Port Stanley landmark and my experience tells me that there would be substantial opposition in the Falklands to such a plan… In addition, there are other factors in public opinion. People in Stanley remember with considerable bitterness the inexcusable loss of the Fennia'*.[78]

Just as the condition of the *Charles Cooper* got rapidly worse, the local interest increased. The hulks were seen as a positive contribution to the islands' tourist attractions. There had been a growth in interest in the islands since the War. It was possible to fly directly from Britain to the new airfield at Port Pleasant and there were a growing number of adventure cruises to the Sub Antarctic. Wild life was the principal attraction, but maritime relics and battle fields had their followers too. By 1991 there was a maritime trail and a guide for the Stanley waterfront and the new museum contained a marvellous display of maritime relics including one of the trail boards of the *Charles Cooper*. However, the Falkland Islands Government's resources were limited and certainly could not stretch to salvage or stabilisation. What made matters worse were two types of marine borers were present in the waters of the harbour — teredo and gribble. The teredo is a wood boring mollusc. A long worm like creature with a tiny shell at its head end. It can eat its way along the grain of a timber. Its tunnels can be as much as half an inch in diameter and it can fatally weaken a timber without leaving any visible sign on the outside. The gribble is a tiny arthropod that burrows into wood and feeds on wood fibres. They leave hundreds of tiny holes making the wood crumbly and weak. The combined efforts of teredo and gribble is highly destructive. For some reason in the late 1990s, they decided to multiply in Stanley and their appetite for wet timber had dire consequences. At first, it was thought that they might have arrived in the ballast water of a visiting vessel. Research showed that all the local inter-island schooners had been copper sheathed to protect their planking against such creatures. In 1895, Harding, FIC's manager, ordered that telephone poles sited below the high tide mark should have their lower part sheathed in nine inches of yellow metal to protect them.[79] More recently, David Eynon of South Atlantic Marine Services was called on to help with replacing wooden piles on the Public Jetty. He kept a sample of one of the old piles which is riddled with teredo bore holes. Teredo were first detected on the *Egeria* by Robert Elliot and Eric Lawson in 1996. In 1998, it and gribble were found on the *Charles Cooper* and by 2002 they were present in large numbers on the *Jhelum* at the upper end of the harbour. The 1998 survey by Merseyside Maritime Museum reported the starboard side was collapsing into the harbour, the bow had been damaged, the roof was buckled and many of the main deck beams had cracked open. It got worse in the following years. The remains of the roof had to be removed in 2001. The risk to people on Ross Road of being hit by loose roofing sheets during gales was too great. By 2002, most the starboard tween decks was underwater at all states of the tide. The main deck beams were smashed and the stanchions collapsed. The port side planking was rotten and crumbling. The bow section remained relatively intact and could with some expense be brought ashore, but it would still need to be conserved and displayed inside a building to preserve it long term. At the time of writing, plans are in hand for just such an operation. Let us hope it is a success.

---

[78] Nicholas Dean to Karl Kortum 19th April 1993
[79] FIC Archives, Colonial Manager's Despatches 11th April 1895